BACK STAGES

The Making Of
Art and Culture

Katrin Korfmann
Jens Pfeifer

CONTENTS

'We are fascinated by systems of manufacture for art and culture as opposed to the romantic notion of the artist labouring in solitude within their studio. By emphasising values placed on the production and handling of artistic goods, we are presenting this work as a visual tribute to the creative process.'

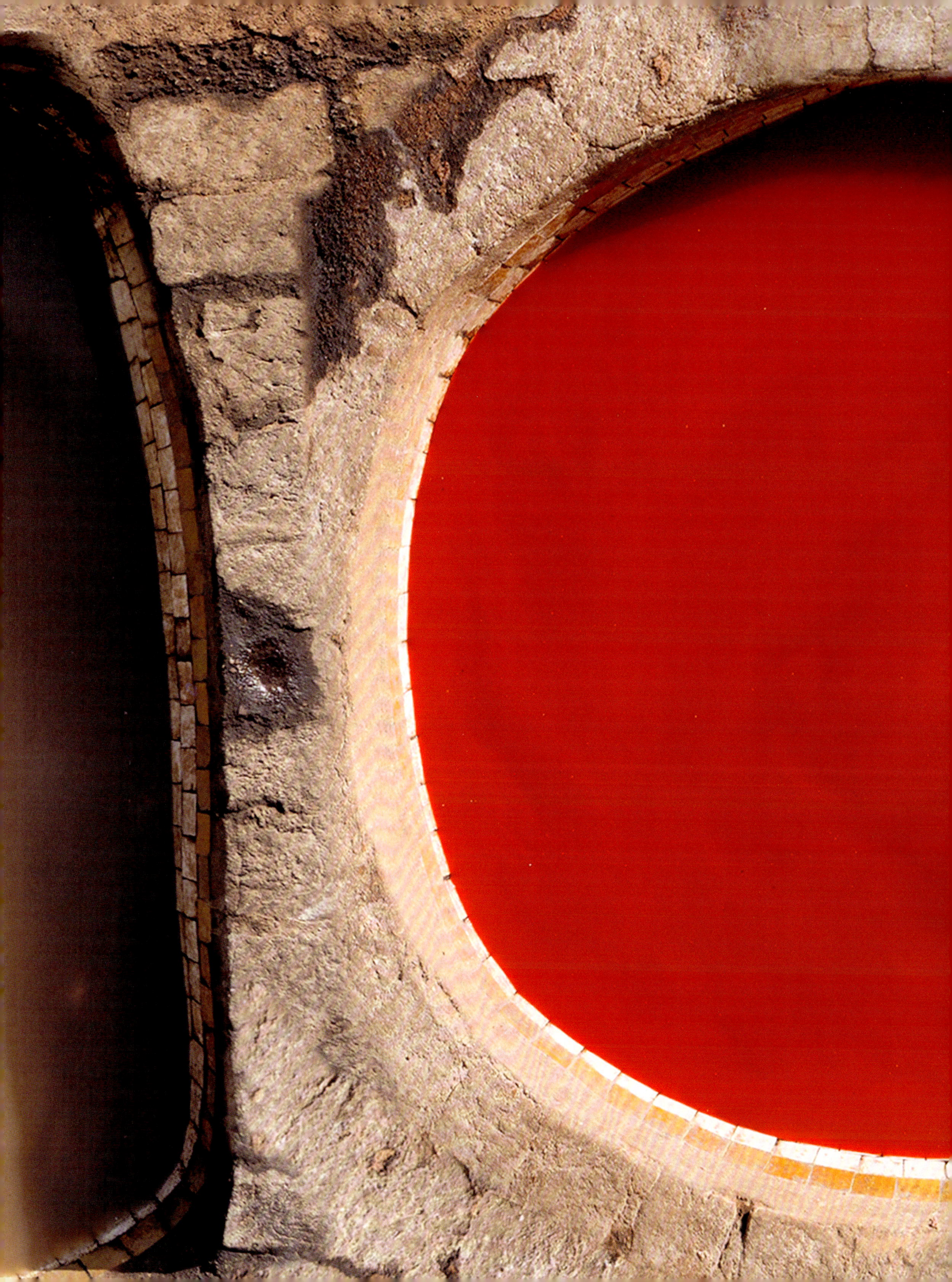

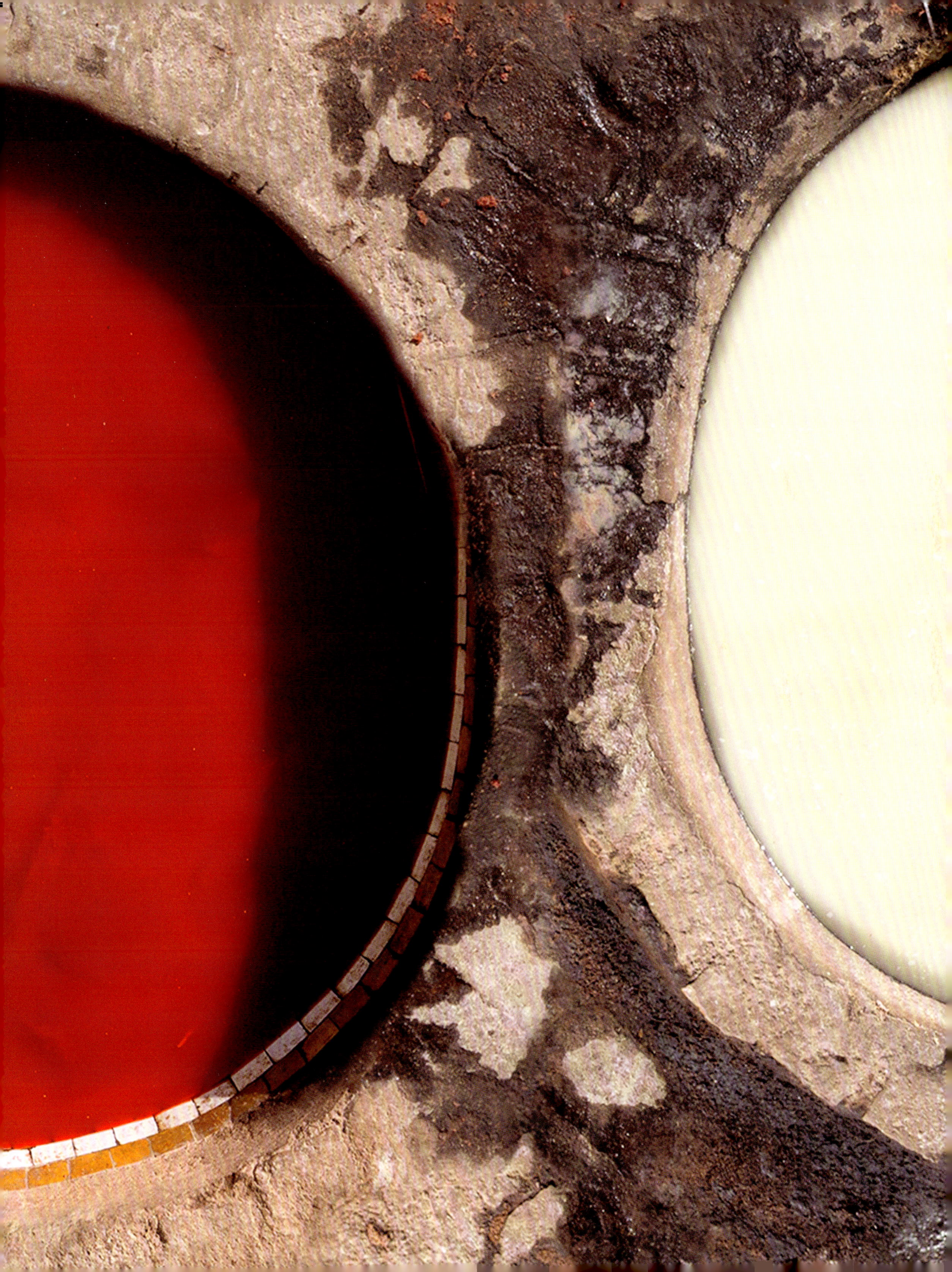

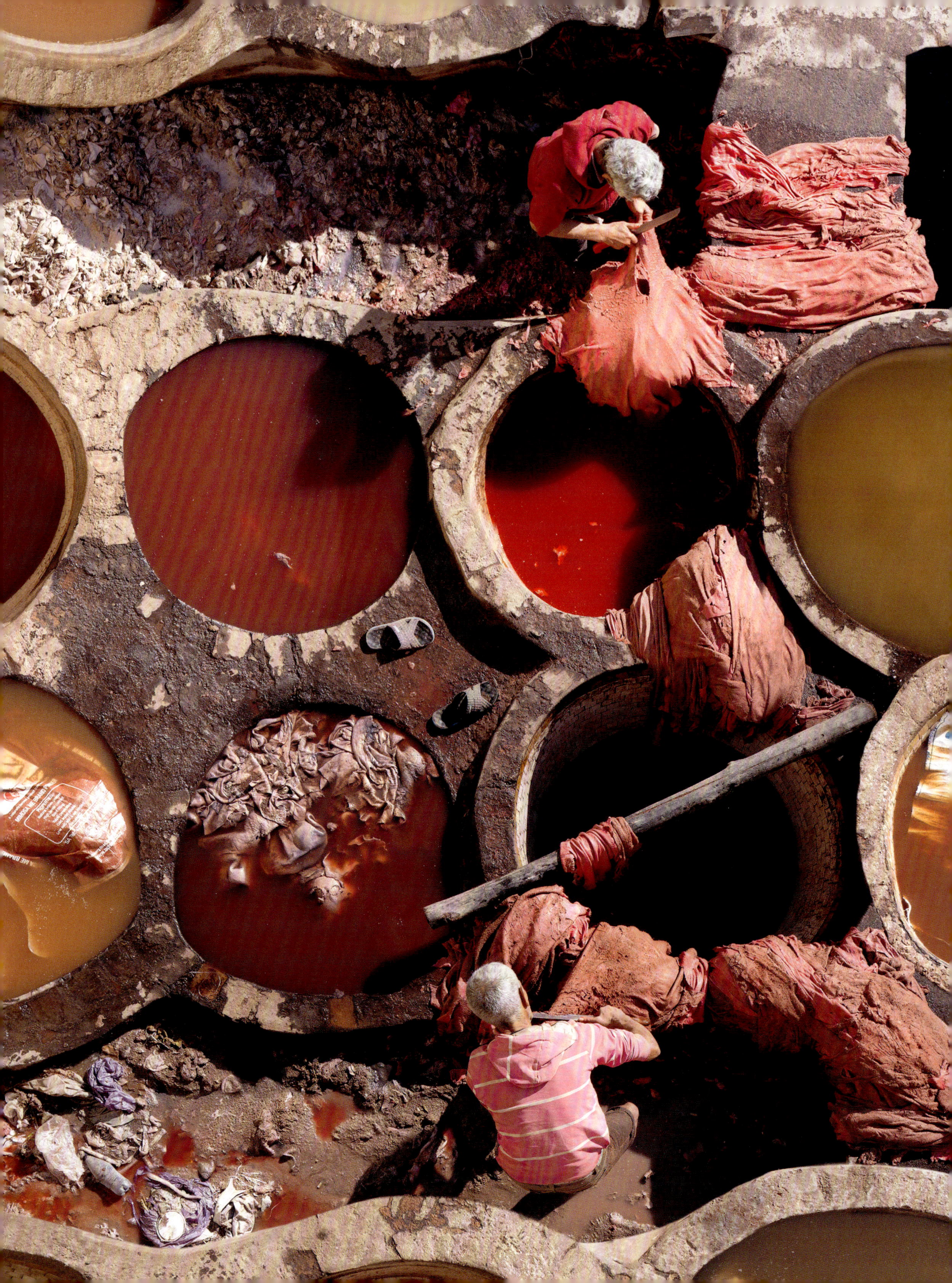

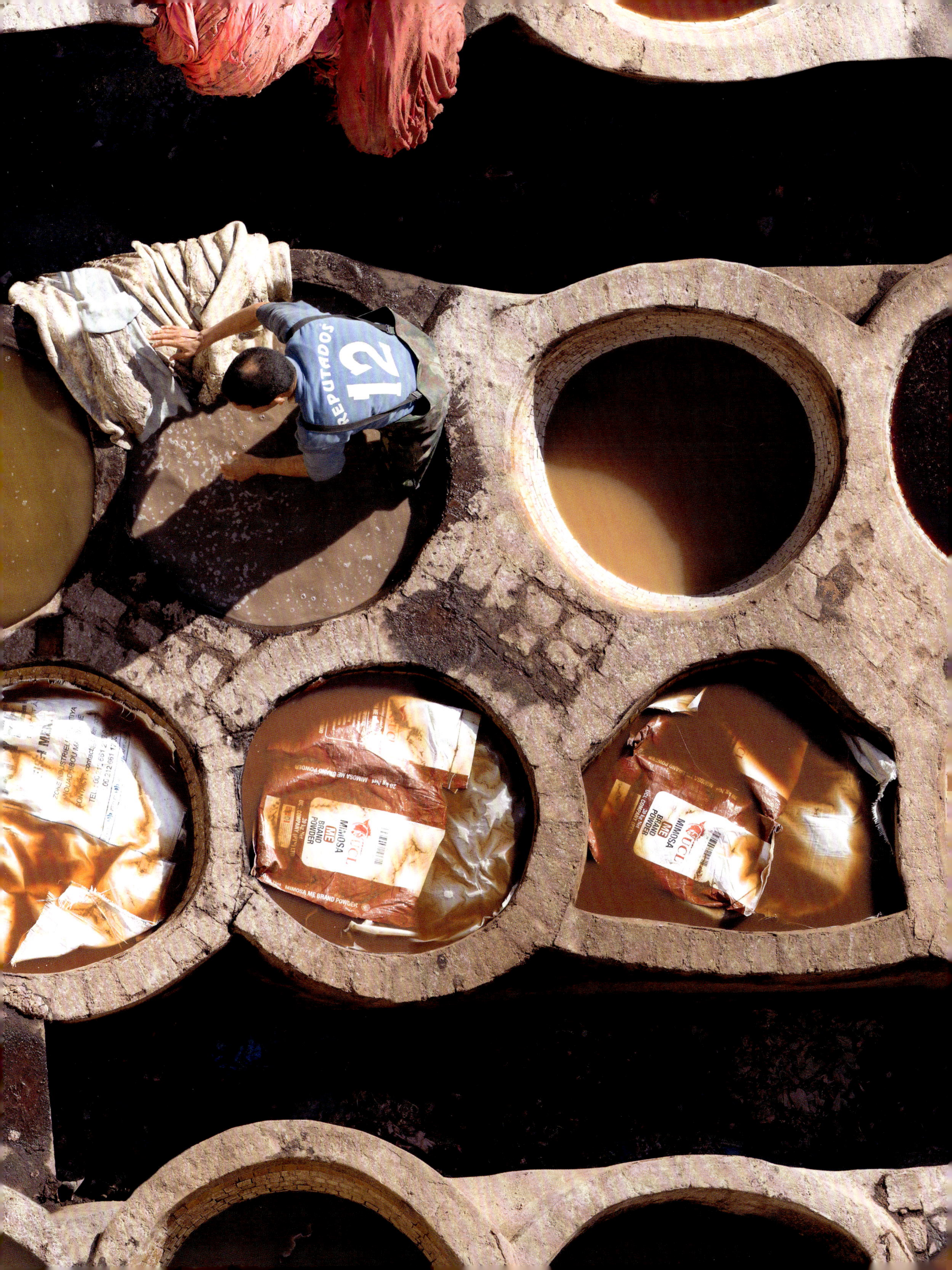
REPUTADOS
12
MIMOSA
ME BRAND
POWDER
UCL
MIMOSA ME BRAND POWDER

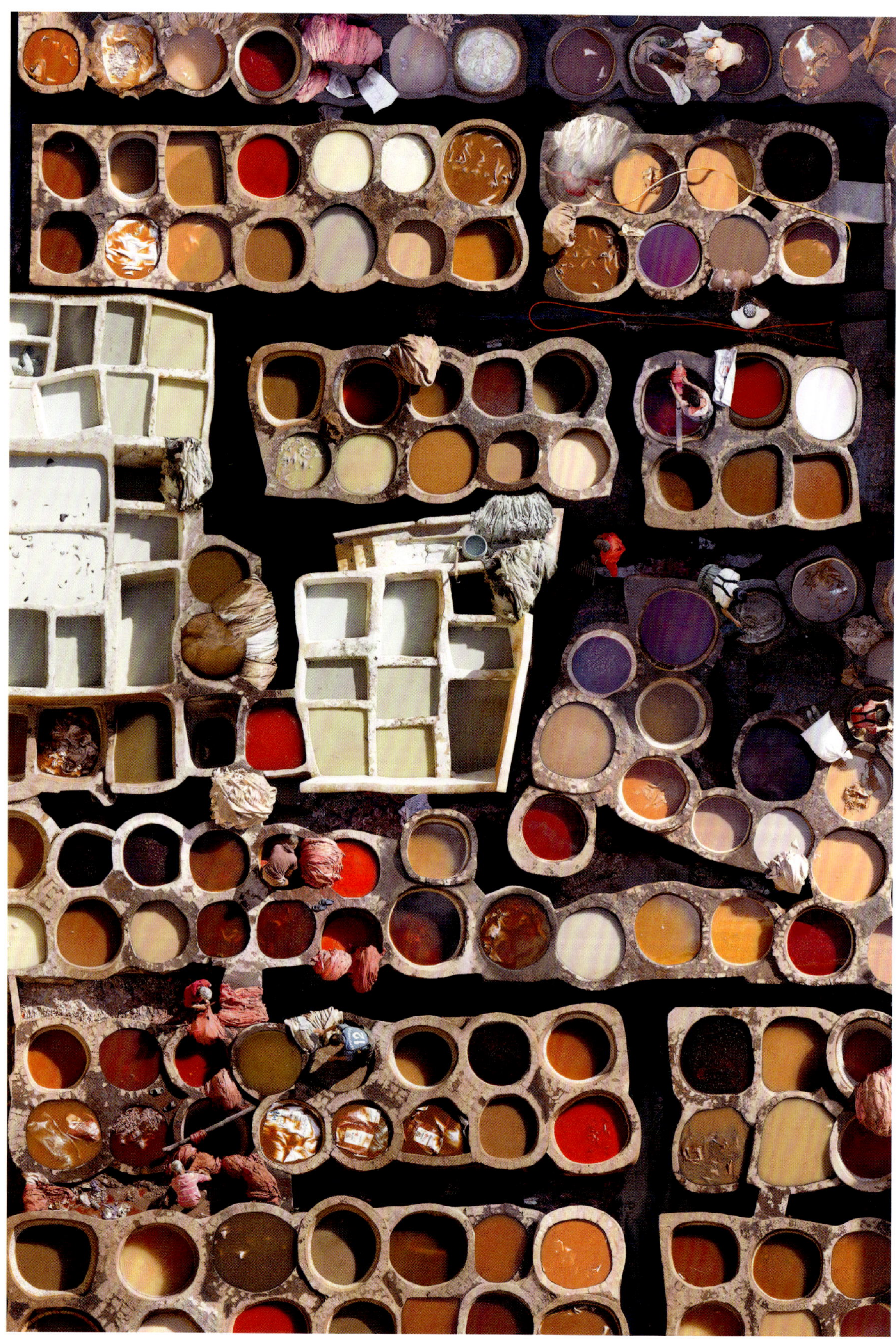

CHOUARA, FEZ
11th-century tannery in Morocco
173 × 120 cm | 68" × 47"

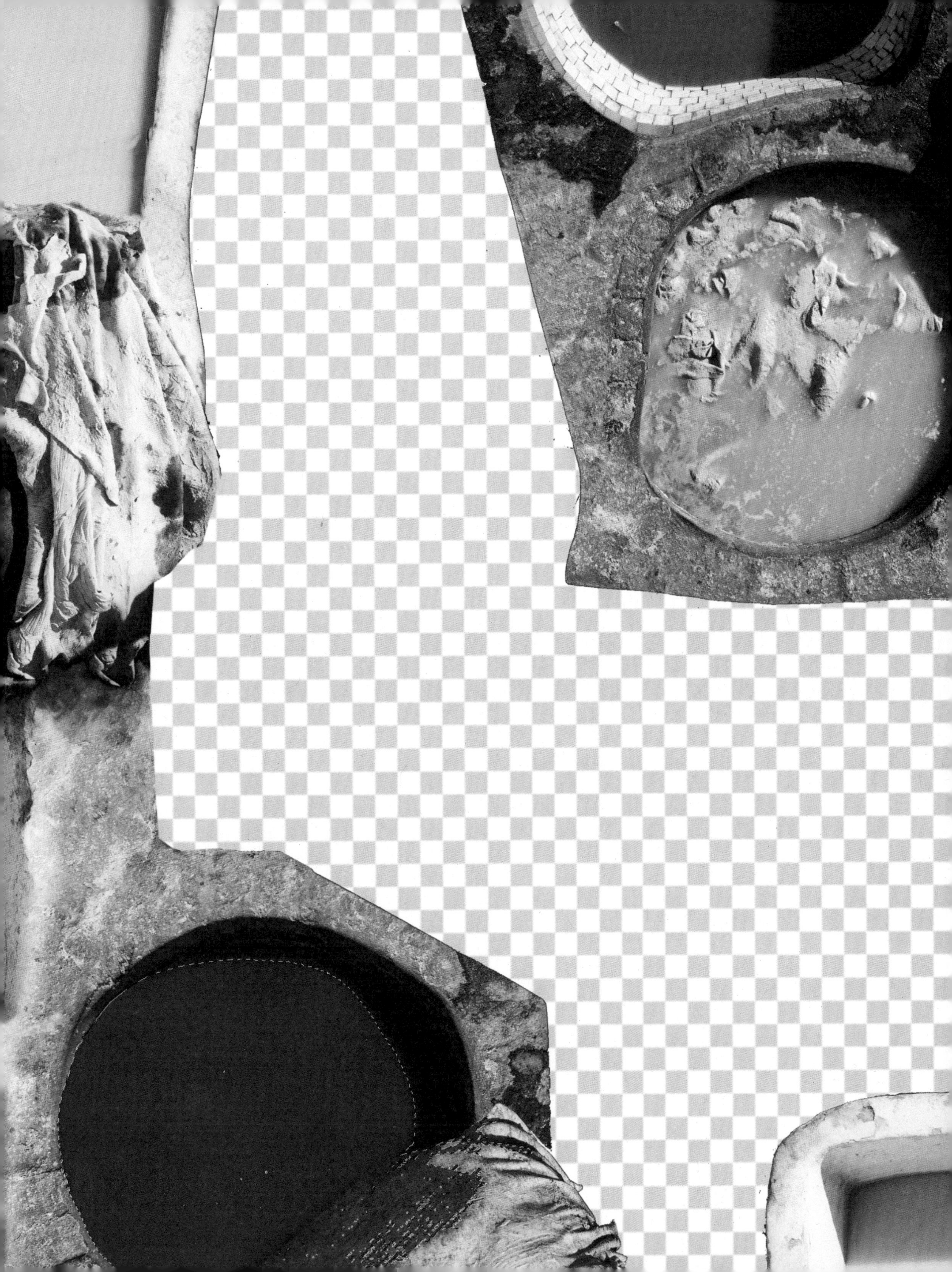

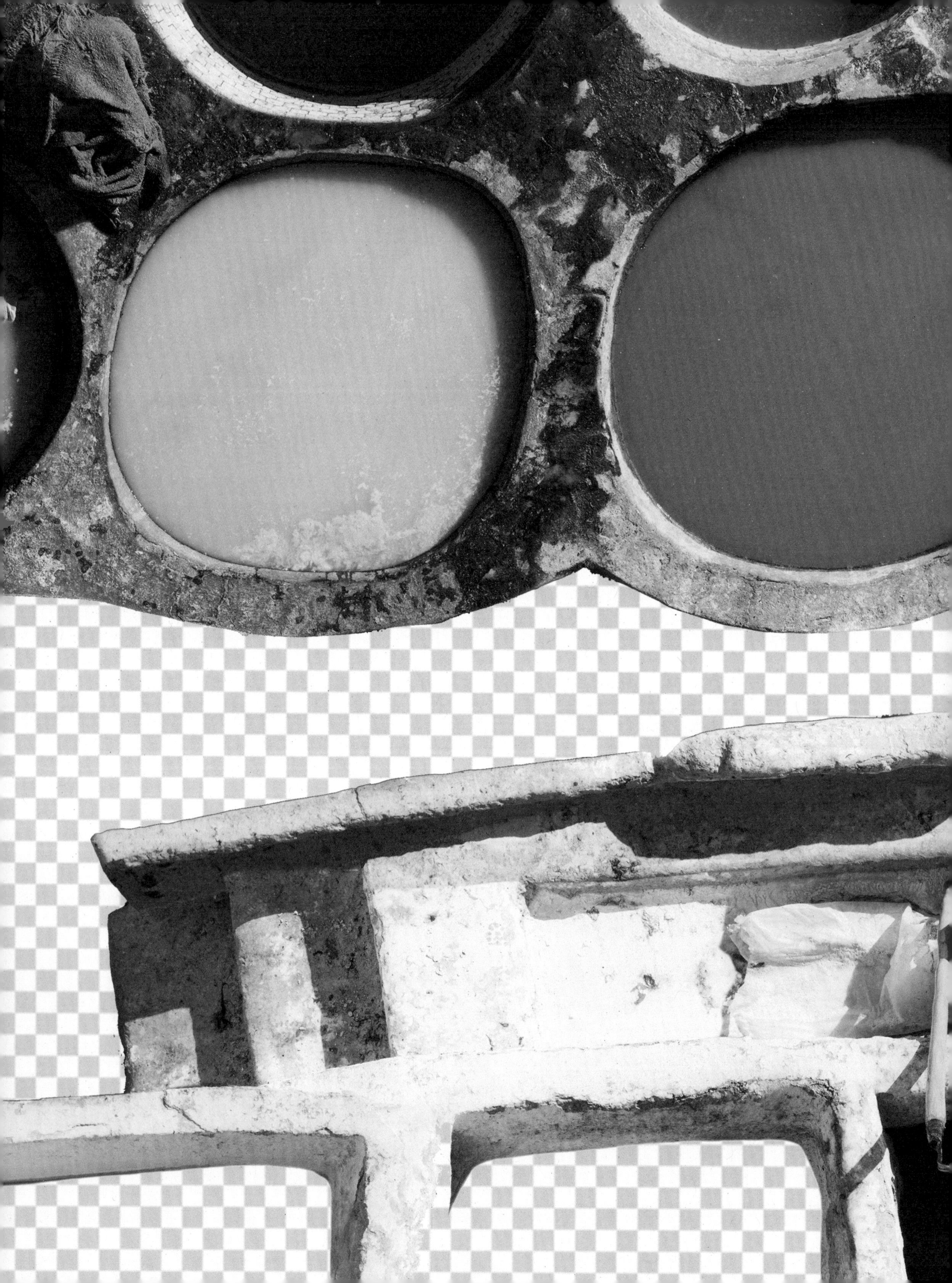

One of the unintended consequences of modern capitalism is that it has strengthened the value of place, aroused a longing for community.
(Richard Sennett)

1.   Initially, the *Back Stages* project tempts me to think about labour. This line of thought isn't odd or implausible. *Back Stages* shows twelve photo-compositions of shop floors all over the world. A small glass factory in the Chinese province of Fujian. A marble workshop in Carrara. A dance studio of the Dutch National Ballet in Amsterdam. A bronze foundry in the Dutch province of Brabant. A tannery in Morocco. Just to name a few.

These are all places of labour. Predominantly heavy labour. Often unhealthy, sometimes dangerous and, outside Europe, certain to be terribly underpaid as well. Such unionistic tendencies are not the first thing to surface though, looking at the compositions. Presenting itself instead is a pleasant, warm sentiment. An invitation to participate in an exchange about labour. Followed by questions about good, desirable labour. Eventually leading to questions about craft and artistic labour.

The twelve photo-compositions that together make up *Back Stages* clearly form a unity. They have been created with a steady, experienced hand, they are the result of adhering to a strict work ethic and method that are solidly grounded in a consistent aesthetical and ethical universe. Clear, not confused. Pleasant, not tormented. Complex, not obvious. Compassionate, not sneaky or malicious. Generous rather than cynical.
I call the works photo-compositions, photo-paintings or photo-performances, because the artists take the montage of various photographic elements as the guiding principle in creating the images.

The artists' unwavering focus creates a sound idea of what constitutes labour in their universe. The unique production sites and their inhabitants, no matter where they are, belong together. Whether they are glass-blowers, archaeologists, stonemasons, museum visitors or artists. They are members of the same guild. A world with universally applicable basic values for labour.

The representation of labour created by Korfmann and Pfeifer shows a collectivity in action. Here, people produce in groups, not in masses and not as individuals. It's a production that is neither Fordist nor post-Fordist. No assembly-line labour in immeasurable halls, but no hyper-flexible individualised task performed at the kitchen table or during a metro ride either. These groups are small, the size of a sports team. The workers demonstrate the basic attitude of their labour, their basic *Gestus*, to employ a Brechtian term, that embodies the artisanal, psychological and sociological necessities of a profession or social role. Or they move around the floor from one place to another. Their lines of direction seem to be clear and deliberate and are meant to support the work of the labourers who are using their attributes to mix the raw materials.

Still, the viewer will need an attentive eye to discern the labour collective in action. A first glance at these photo-paintings doesn't identify the labourers as the main characters but the shop floor instead. The labourers are concealed in a landscape with an uneven floor that is littered with tools, electrical wires, kilns, tubs, cloths, half-finished or final products. All the equipment needed to arrive from the raw materials to the products that are made in the workshops.

The shop floor imposes itself, massive and monochrome in its roughness, its vulnerability and historicity. Most of these floors have been in use for a long time. They seem to be drenched in the sweat, blood and tears of previous generations. It is noteworthy that the floors in the artists' studios are least inclined to step into the limelight. There, it's the artists who draw the attention to themselves or their equipment. In any case, the floor is always a canvas for a landscape in which labour unfolds. In which labour leaves its traces.

　　　　　　PAUL DE BRUYNE

No matter how concealed the labourers seem to be at first, they can still be recognised as socialised individualities. Only in a split second perhaps, at the edge of the scene, or buried deep down in a detail, but still, as individual people. You see a sweat stain on a man's T-shirt and you start thinking of the way he smells, you wonder how he washes his clothes or if someone does it for him, you think about his wages, his children, his family.
A woman bronze founder is a reminder that this project shows mainly male labourers. (Hold on for a second. Is that actually true? Fact-checking with the artists learns that the number of men and women hidden under the hats in the Chinese glass workshop is roughly the same and that the Chinese granite workshops traditionally employ a lot of women.) But still. Does the female bronze founder do the same work as her male colleagues? Does she receive equal wages?
Someone is wearing a football shirt with number 12, in the fresh blue colour of Manchester City. Would he be a fan, or did he buy or get it for no particular reason? Or could there be a Portuguese team (since the text on the shirt is in Portuguese) that sports the same blue outfit as Man City?

The labour processes in *Back Stages* share a fierce intensity. No matter how dishevelled, even dangerous some of the work spaces appear to be, you never feel as if anyone here is wasting time or money. The space, the people and the materials have a way of finding each other in an intense encounter. The necessity of the work process is prominent. There is not a single trace of carefree idleness.

This intensity in itself implies an exceptional intimacy as well. The space, the materials, the attributes and the people in the compositions belong together, as if they were a family. No one and nothing can do without the other. The intimacy is not only interactional between the labourers, but even more clearly between labourers, space, tools and attributes. Nothing exists outside the work plan, everyone seems to be responsible for it. They are Latourian network worlds, or Buddhist everything-is-connected-to-everything-else realities if you like.

The intimacies on these shop floors are of a particularly physical nature. Palpable. Smellable. Audible. After all, we are dealing with artisanal work here. It's intimate, physical labour that allows for secret knowledge to be shared. From body to body. From hand to hand. Each part in the process implies and involves the other roles. Acting together they create the oeuvre. The work.

My interpretation of *Back Stages* is provoked by the way the photo-performances are framed. They are not images from large factories but from small (family) businesses or artistic production companies. These small businesses are undoubtedly part of larger and more complex networks of acquisition, product development, presentation, PR, distribution and sales, but the image you are looking at reveals a closed, spatially confined, unisonant community. A theatrical scene staged by the artists with the frame of the photo-composition erected around it like a proscenium arch.

Back Stages creates images of collective, intense, intimate, familial, knowledge-sharing and knowledge-generating, strictly delineated spaces, where work is produced in an artisanal fashion.

Would this be the hallmark of good, desirable labour? The question arises from the pleasant feeling, the tranquillity and the invitation to a dialogical vision that I experienced when I first encountered the photo-compositions. The smile they provoked. The friendliness. A perfume of spirituality... Would it have been Korfmann and Pfeifer's intention to paint a utopian picture of labour? A way out of the torture pit of work relations that lead to our collective depressions and burn-outs?

That question inevitably engenders a wider political and societal reasoning.

       PAUL DE BRUYNE

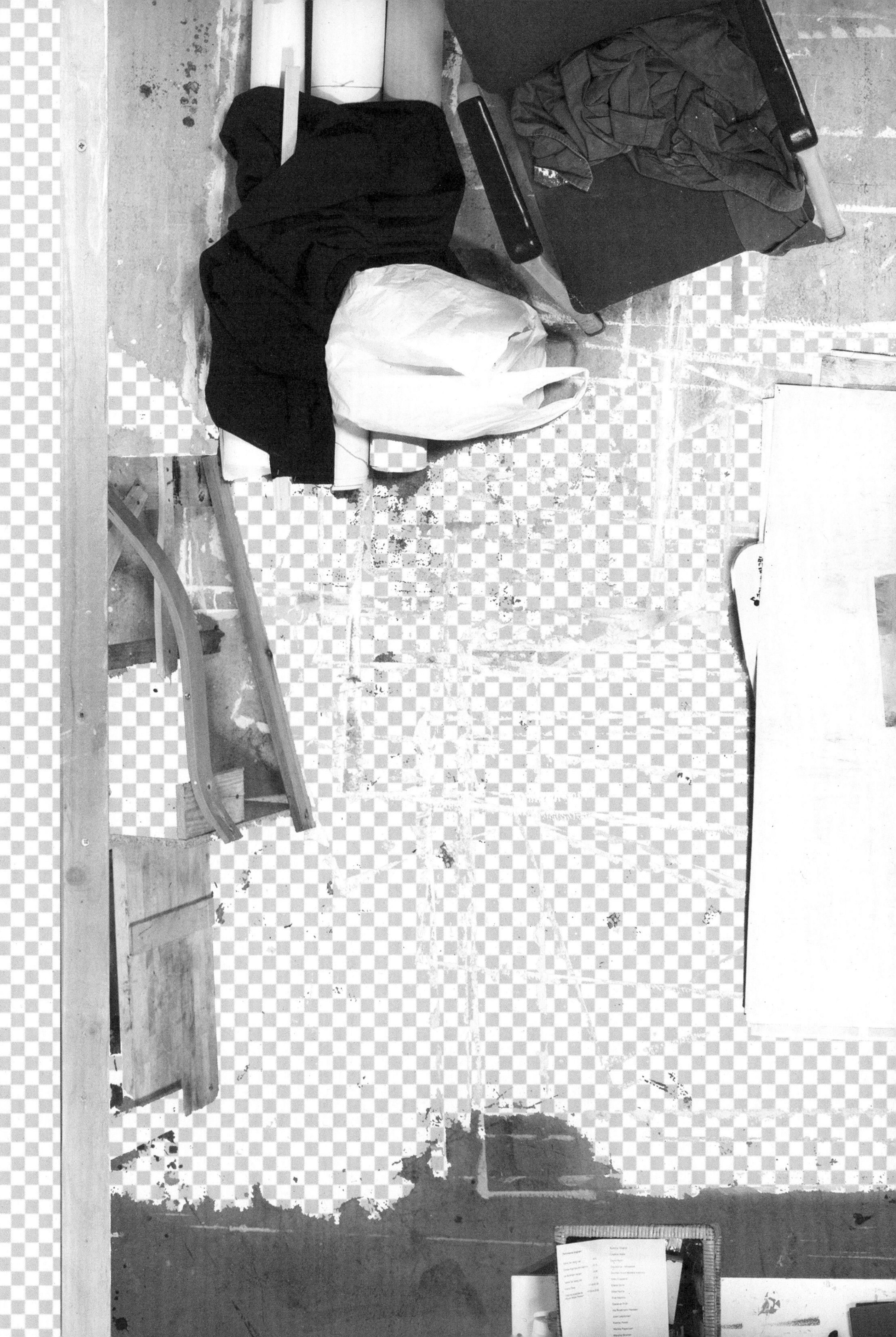

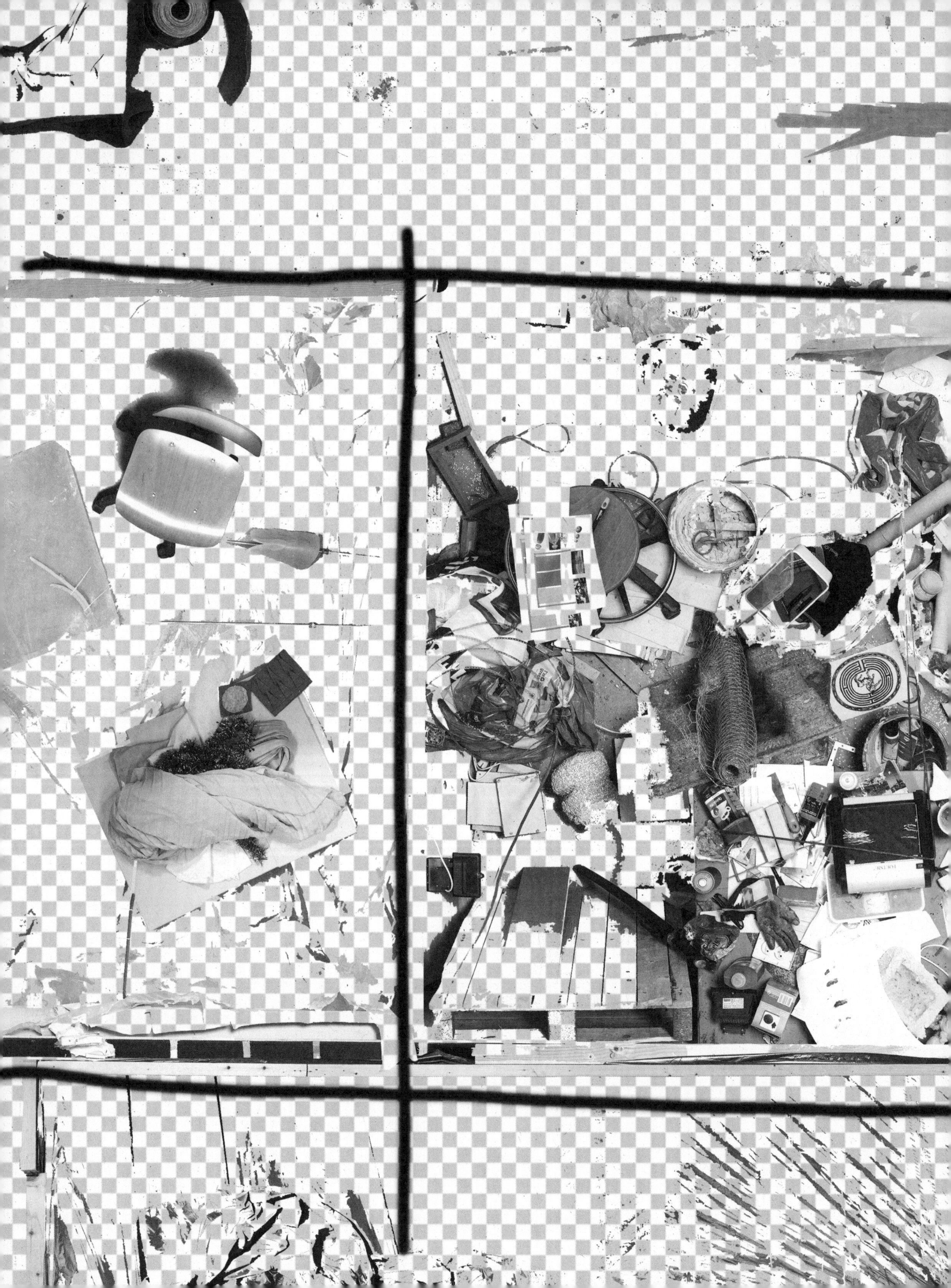

RIETVELD ACADEMIE, AMSTERDAM
Art academy in the Netherlands
173 × 120 cm | 68" × 47"

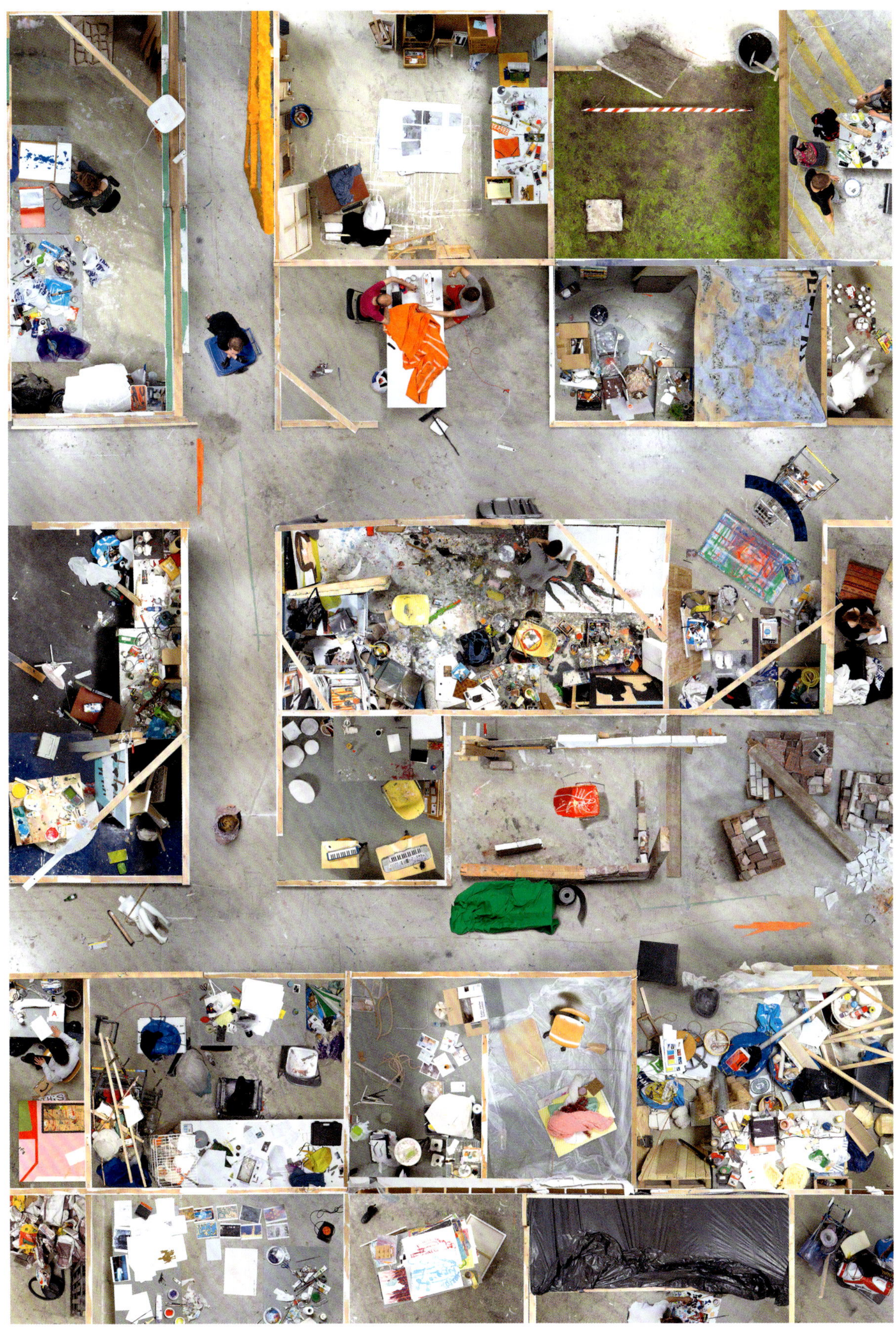

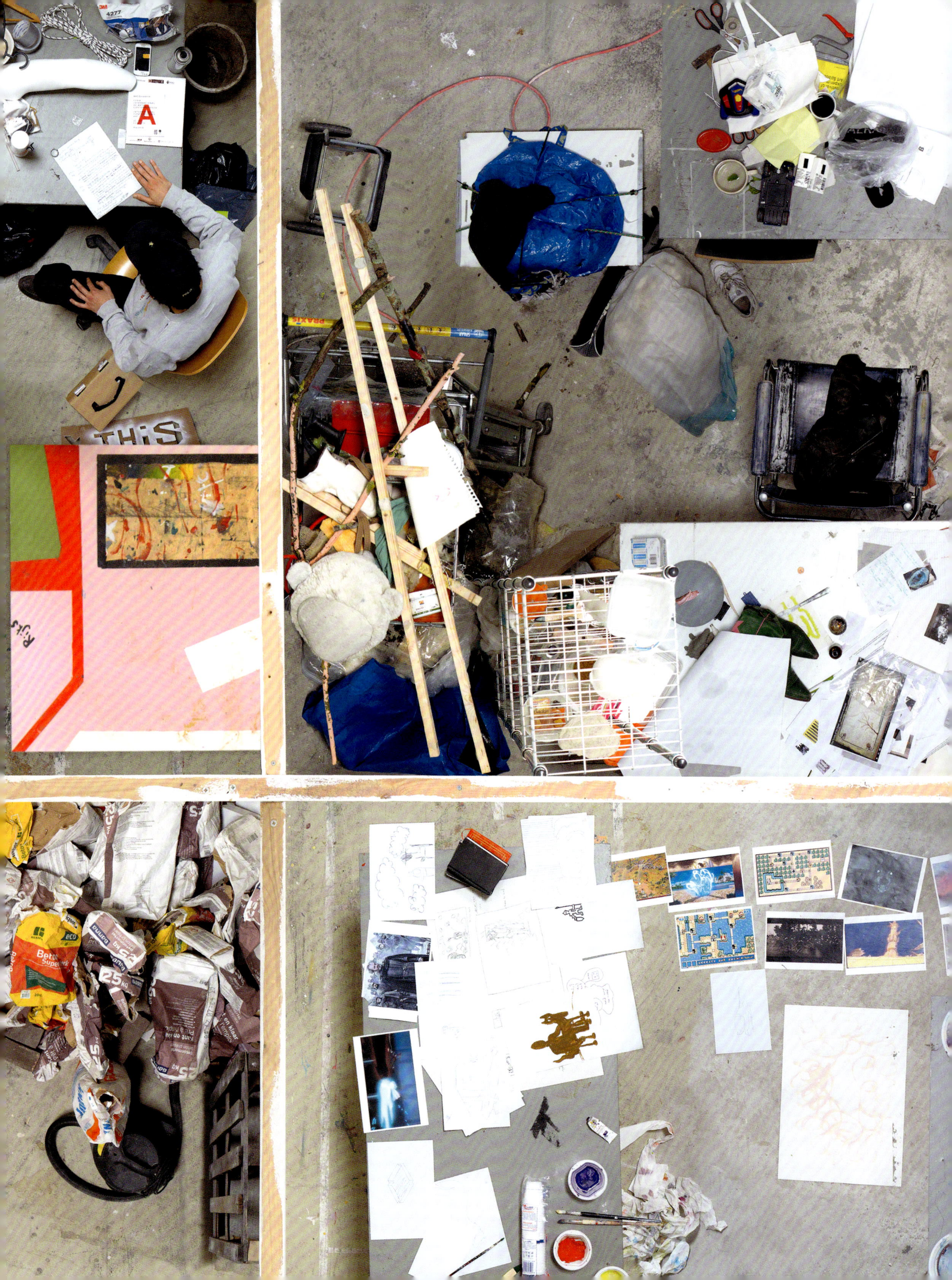

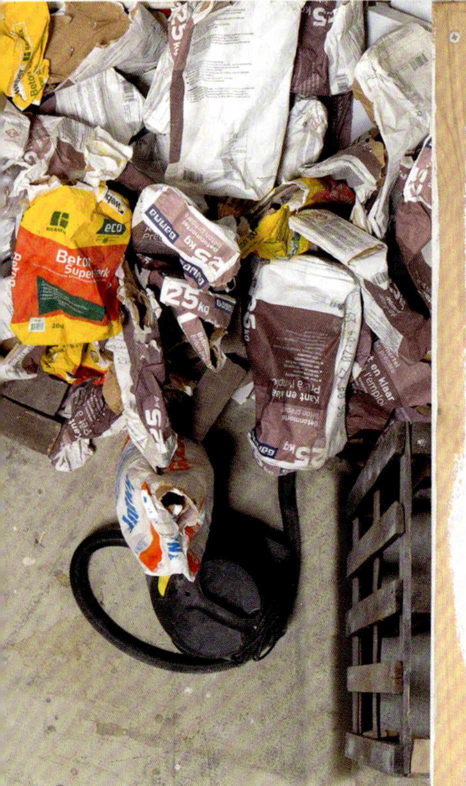
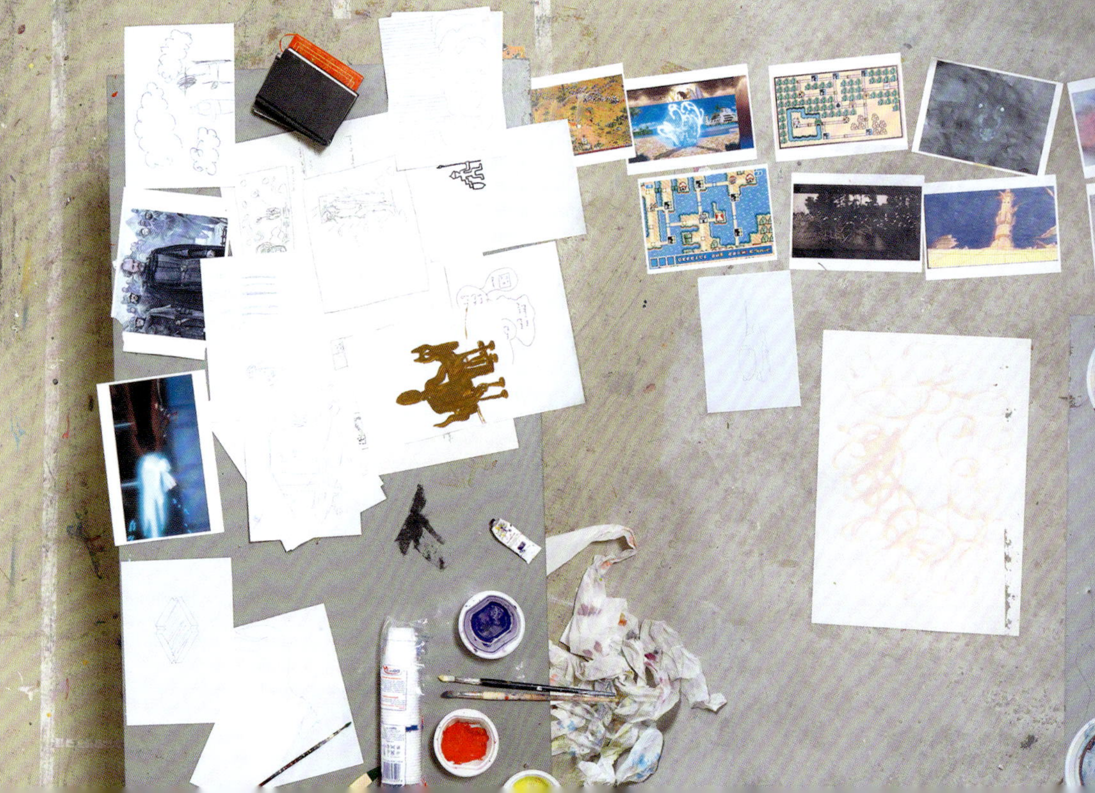

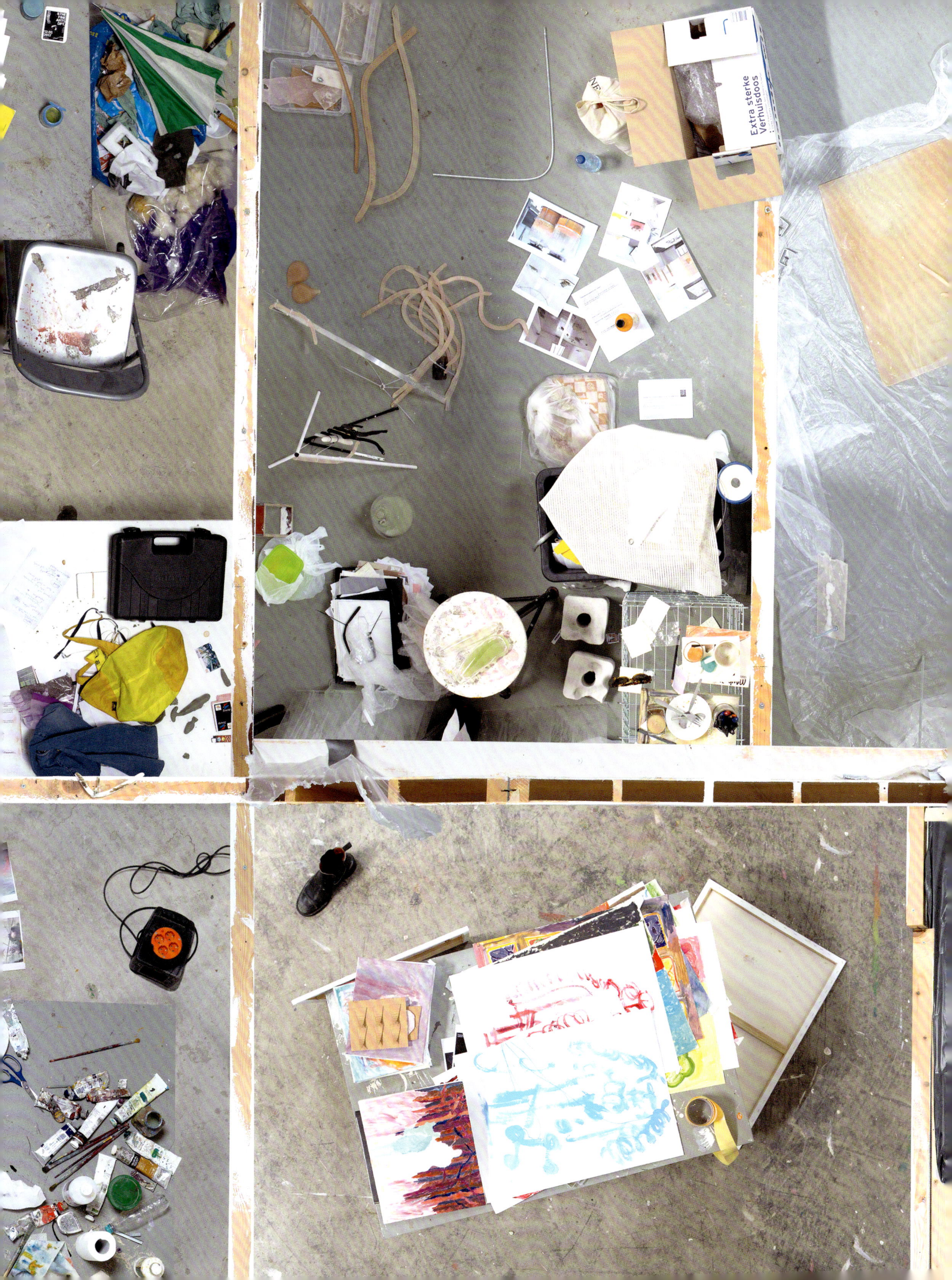

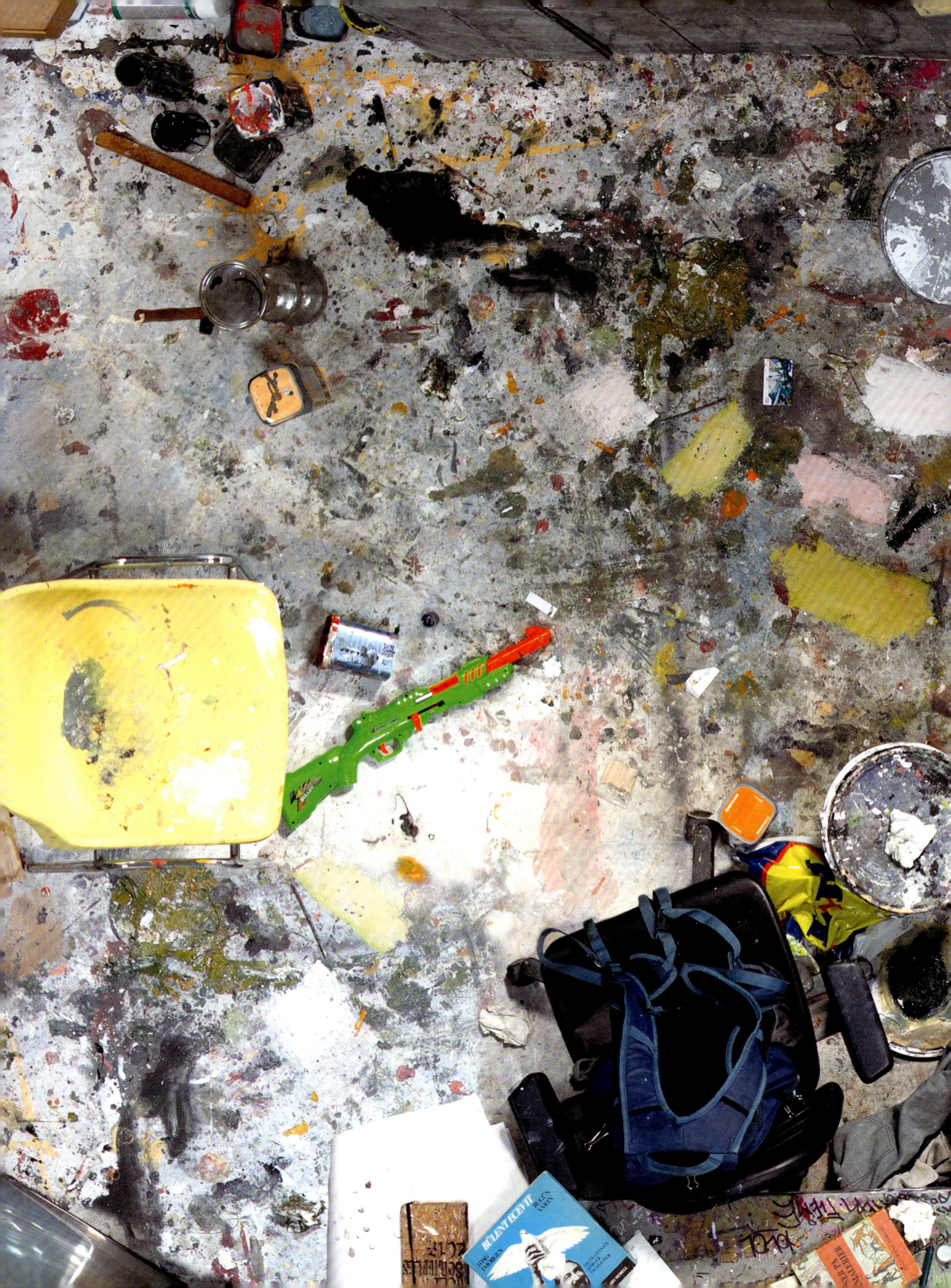
BÜLENT ECEVIT
BUGÜN YARIN

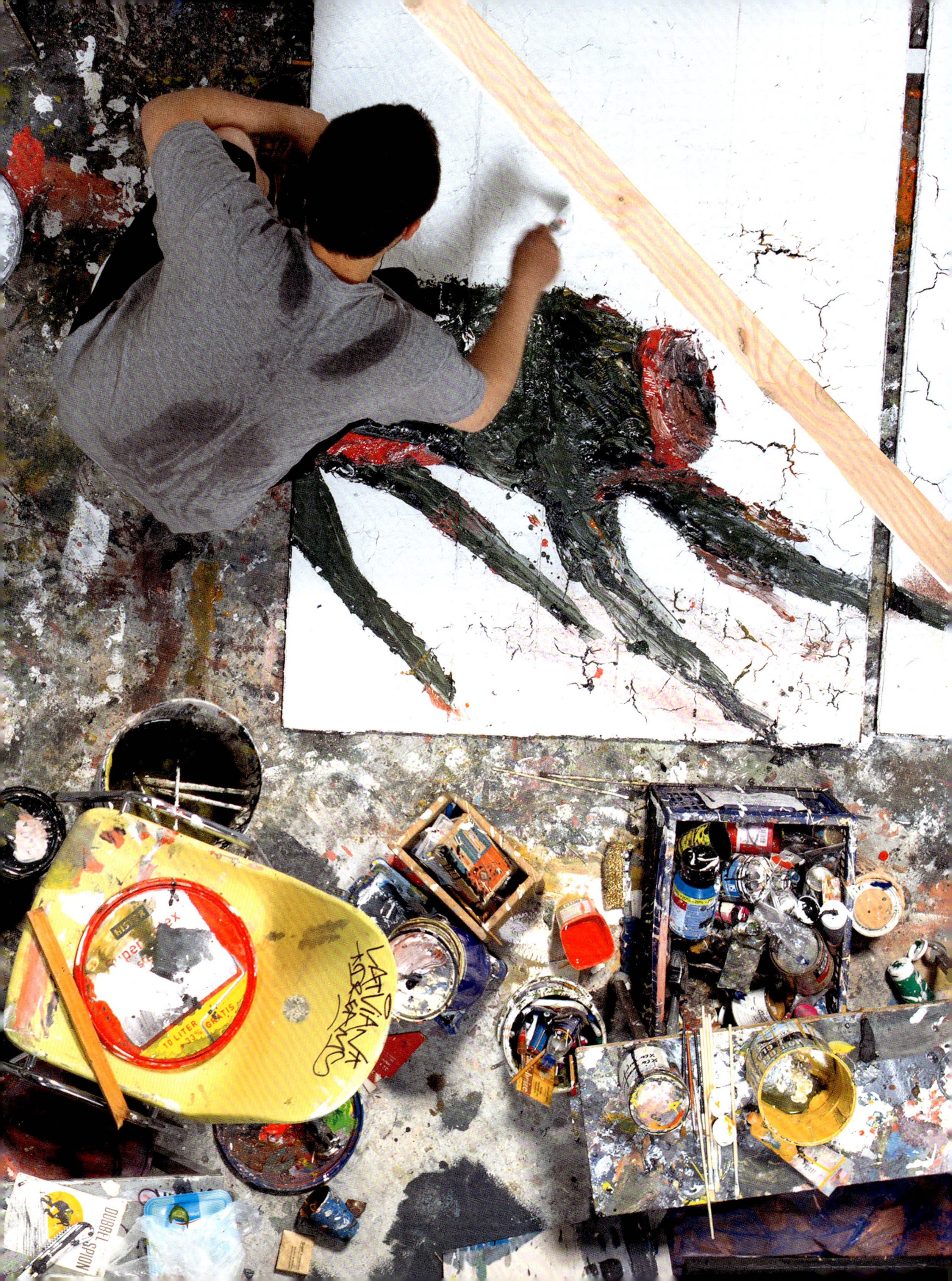

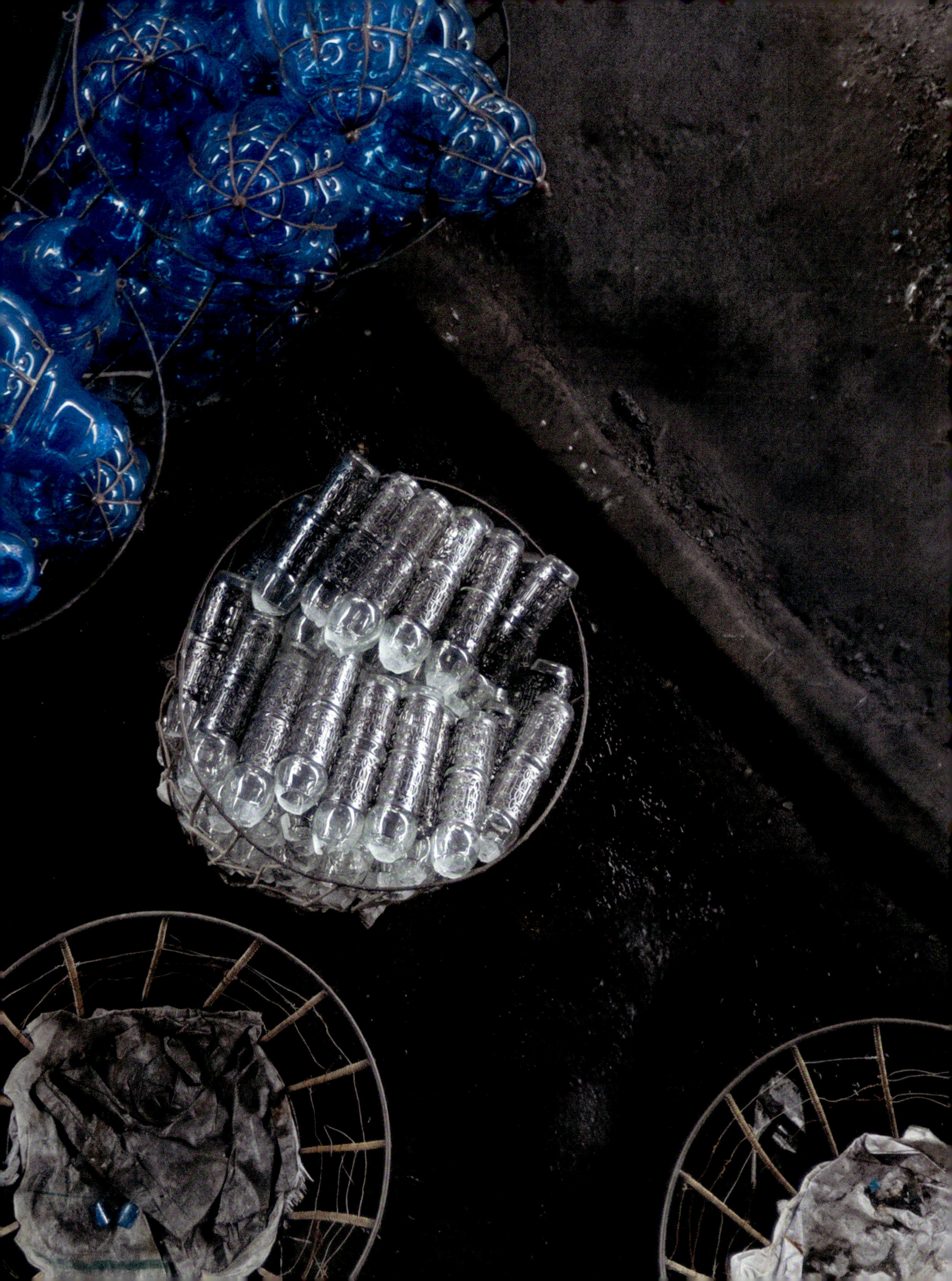

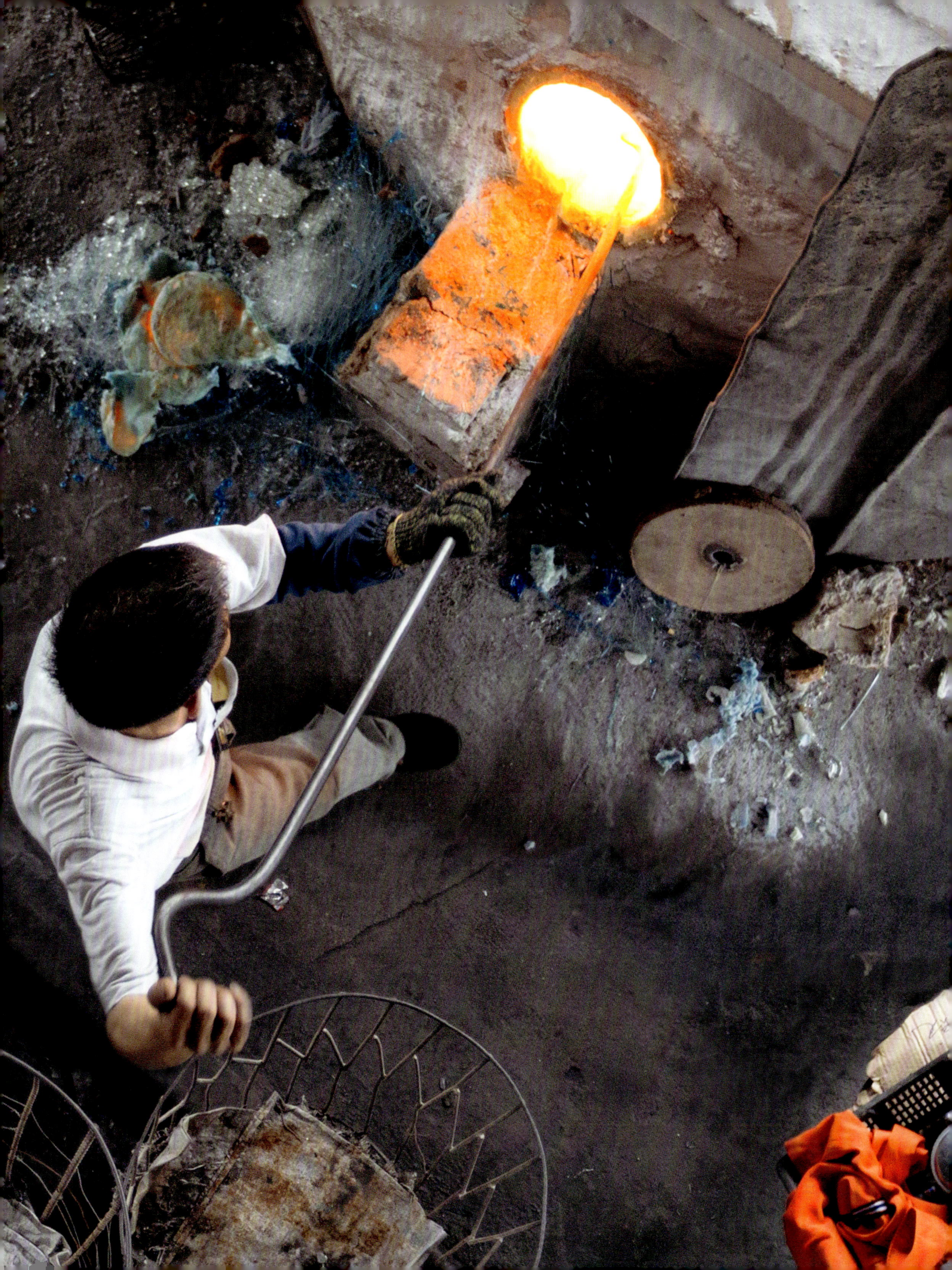

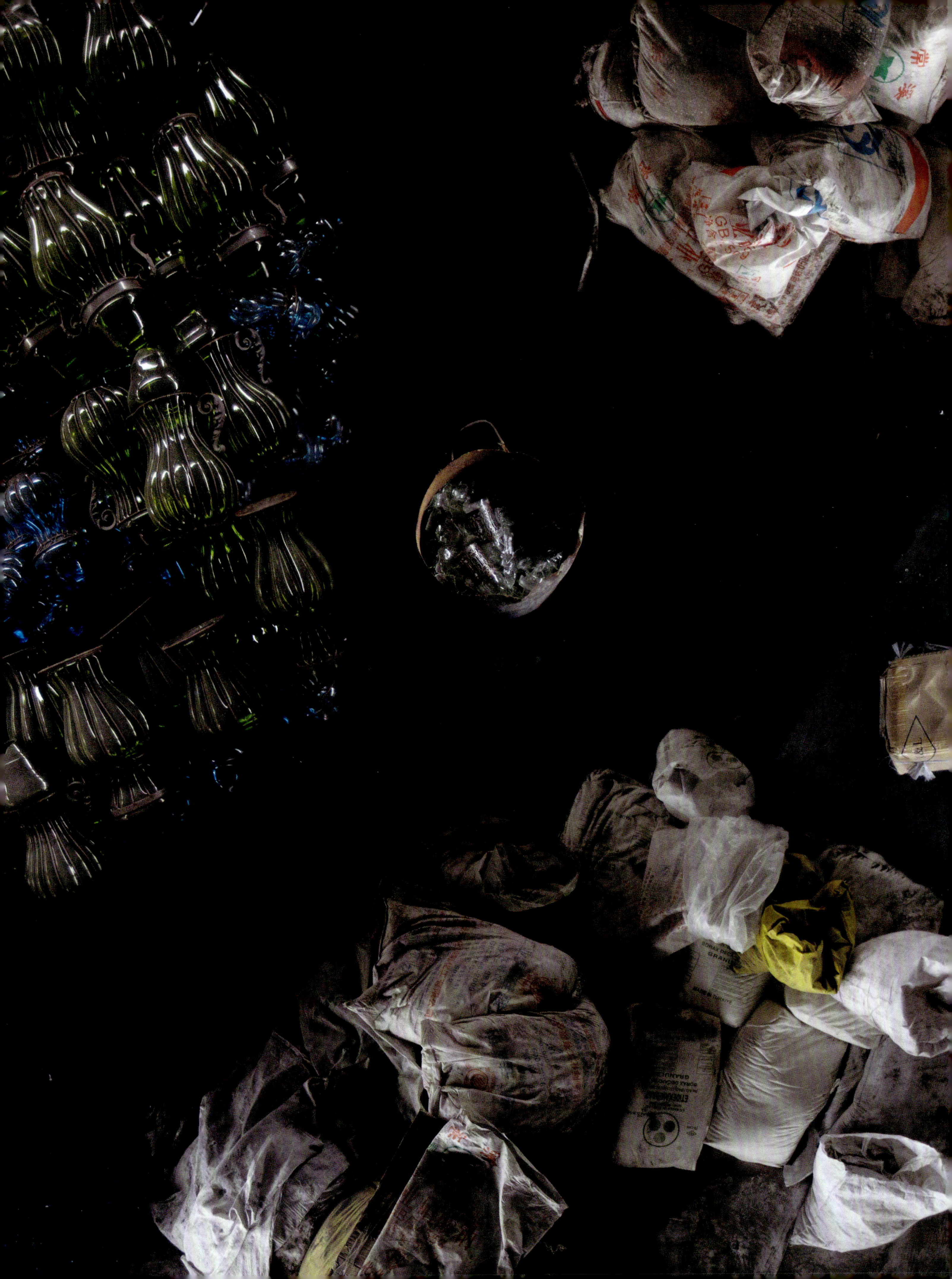

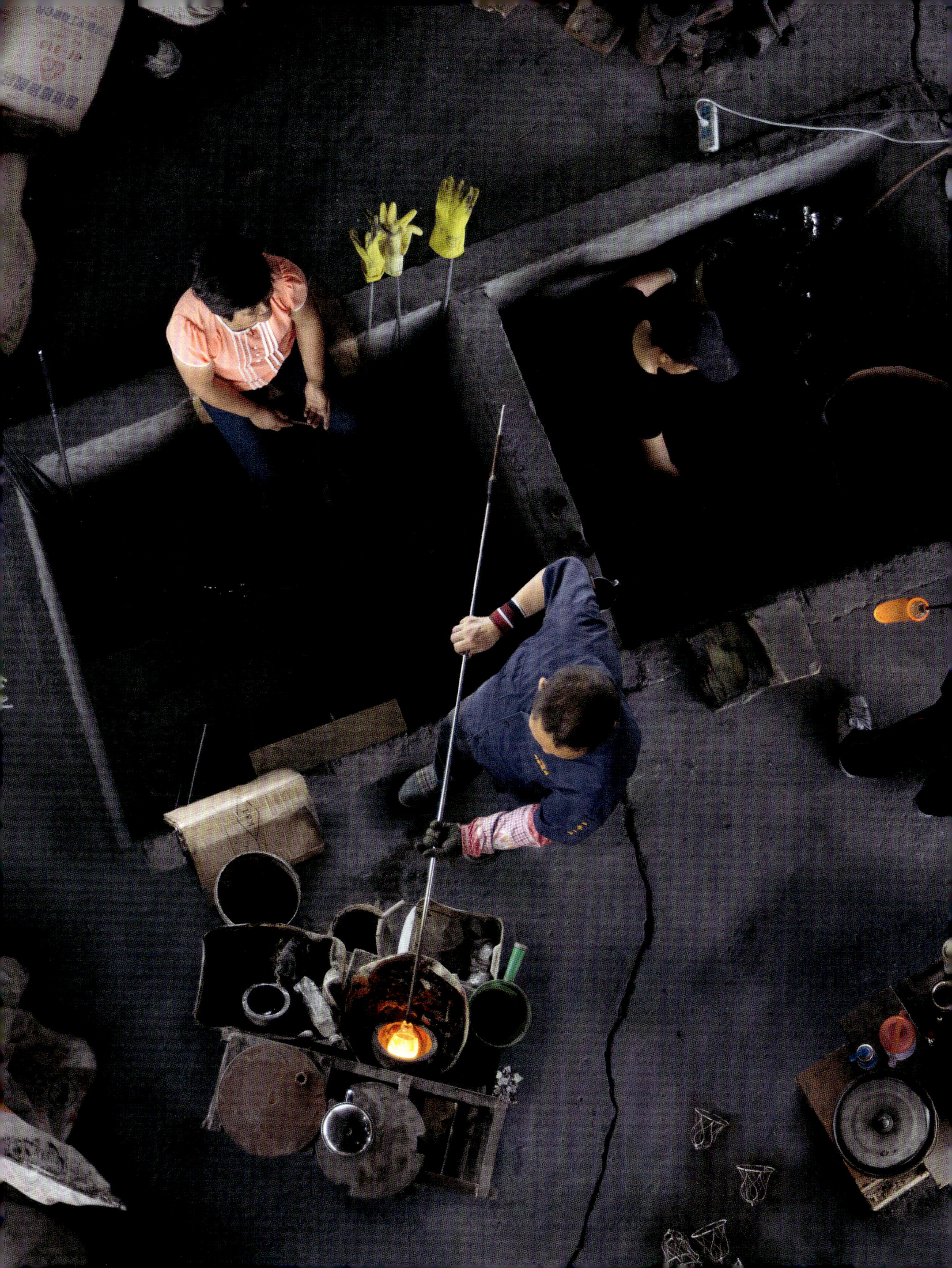

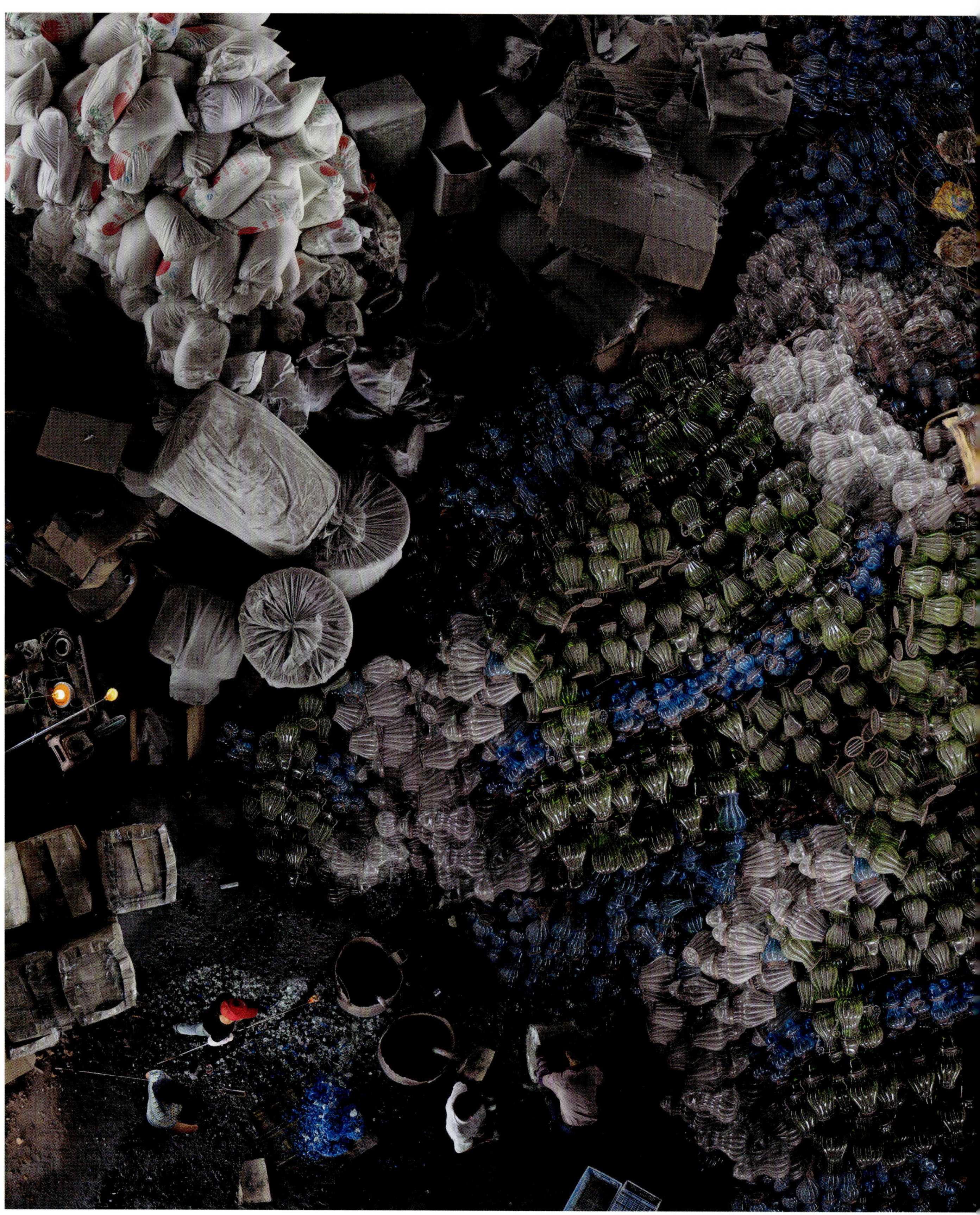

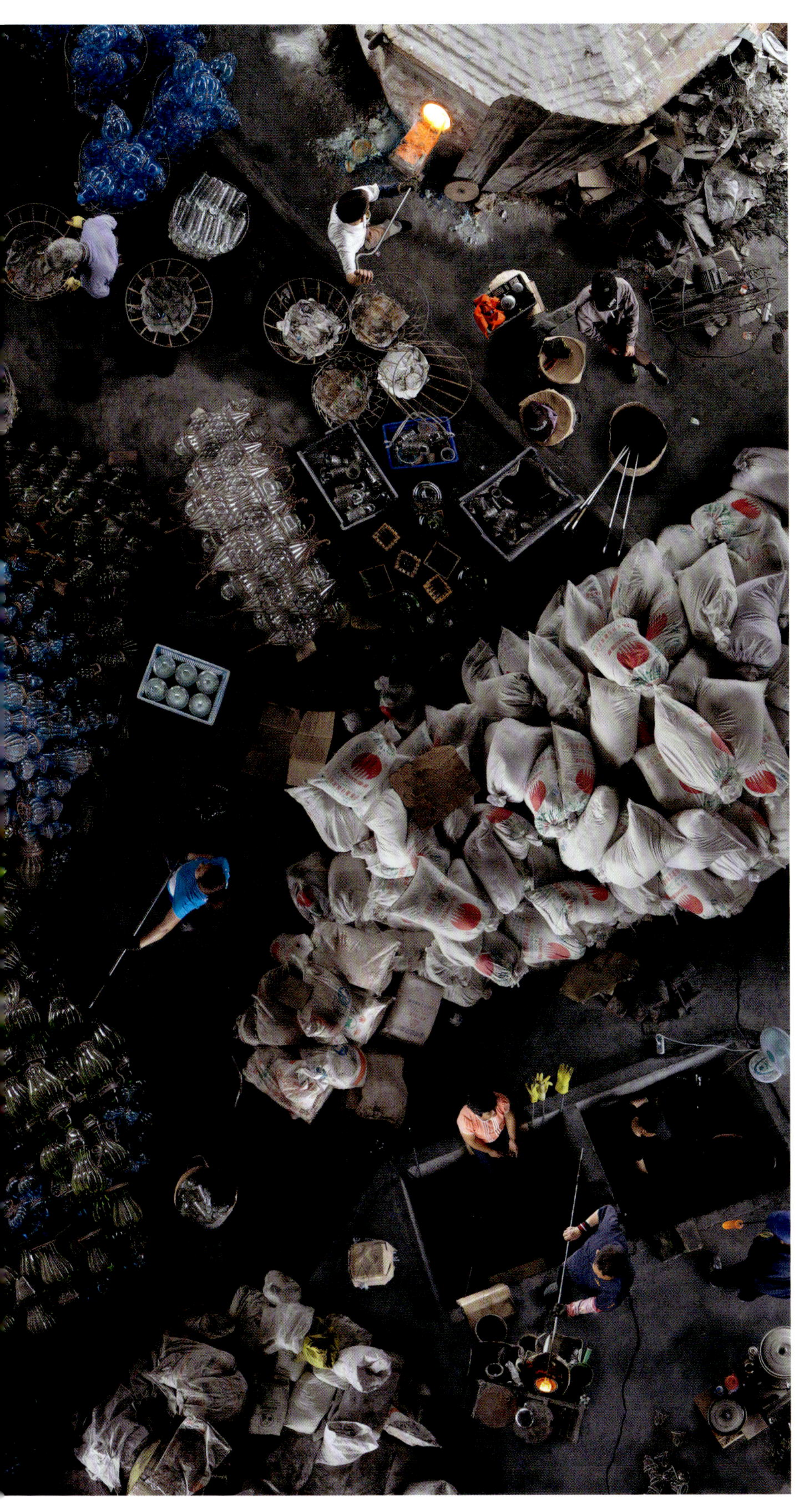

GLASS, ANXI
Glass factory in China
150 × 216 cm | 59" × 85"

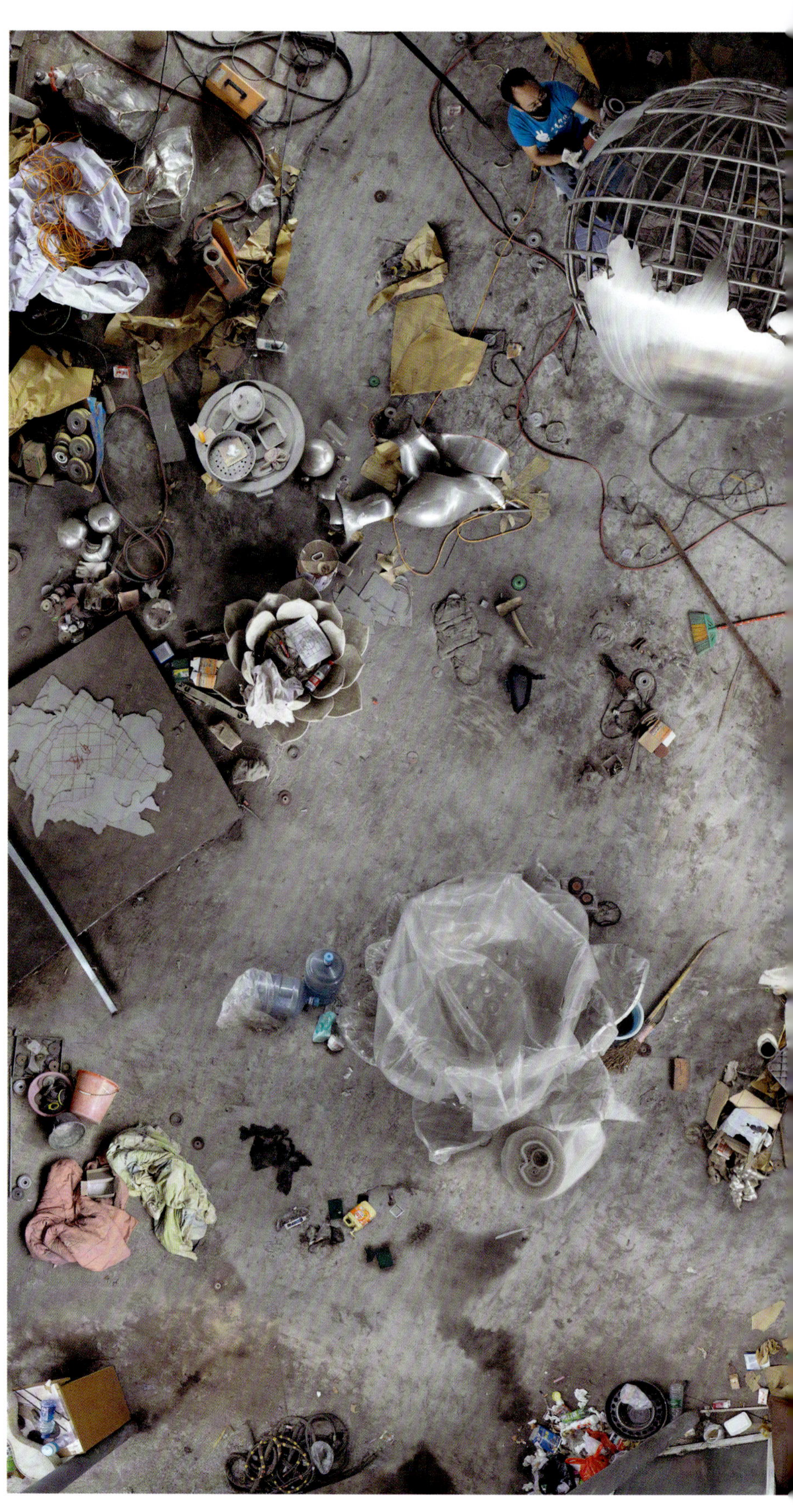

STAINLESS STEEL, XIAMEN
Stainless steel fabrication workshop for sculpture in China
120 × 173 cm | 47" × 68"

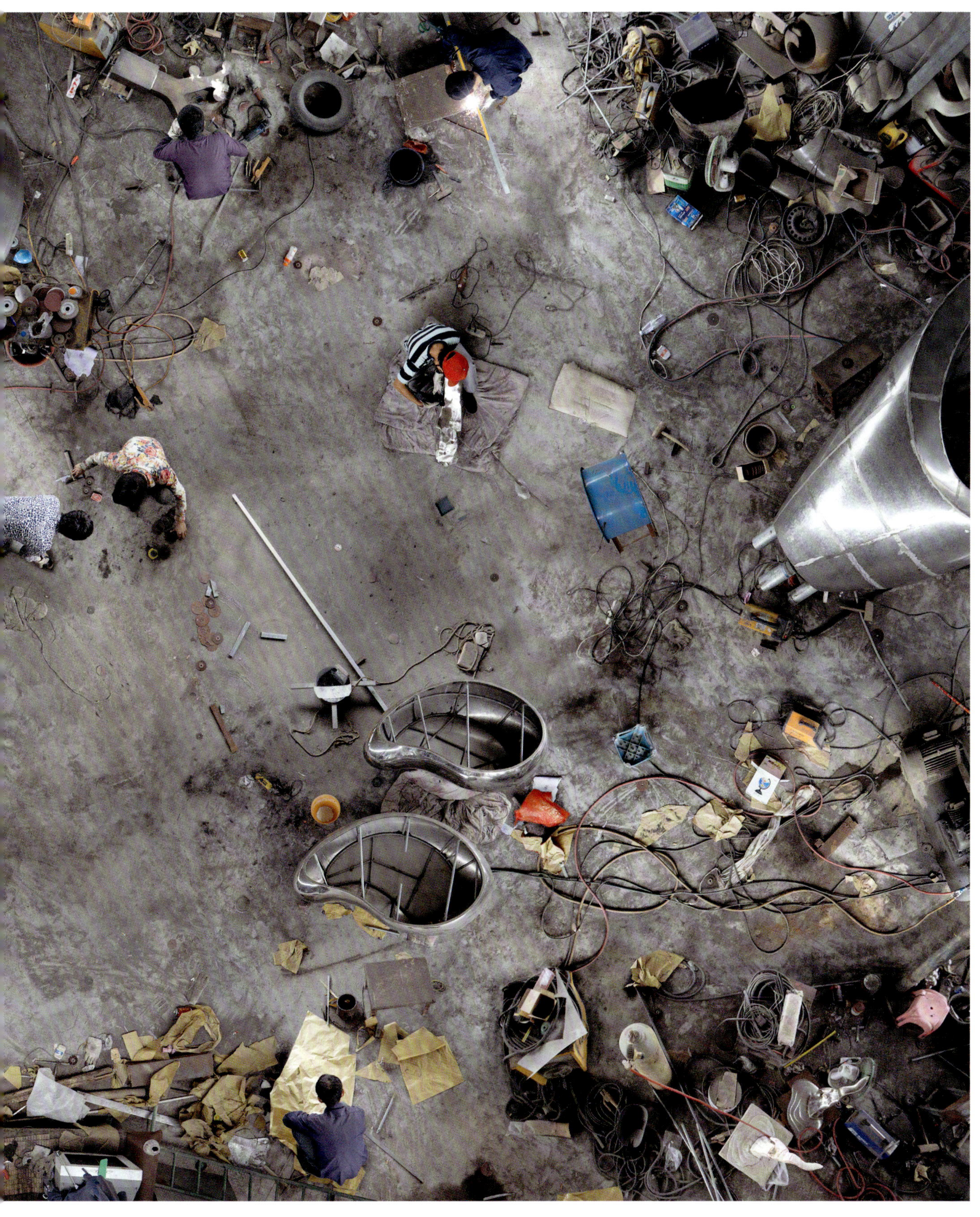

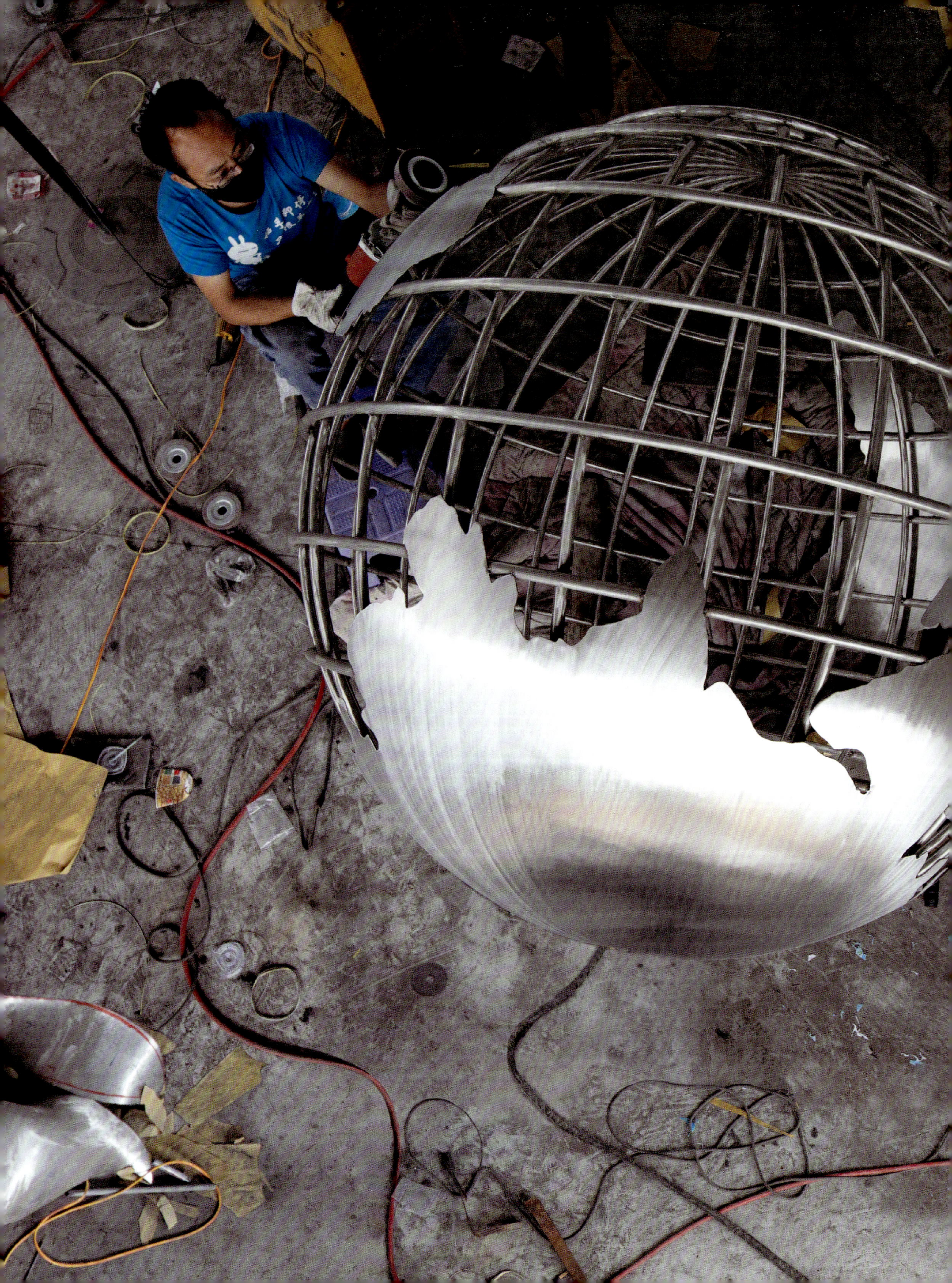

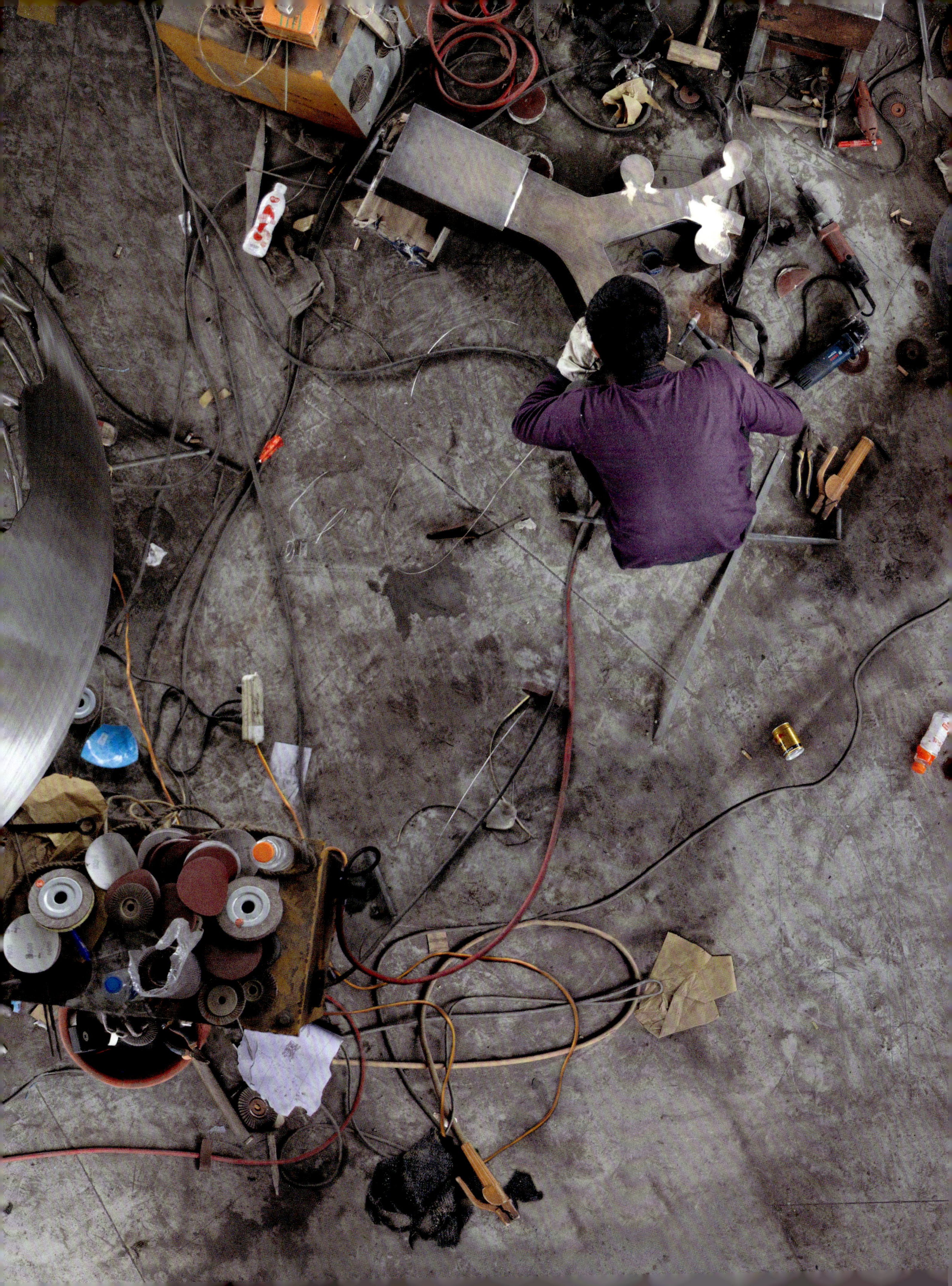

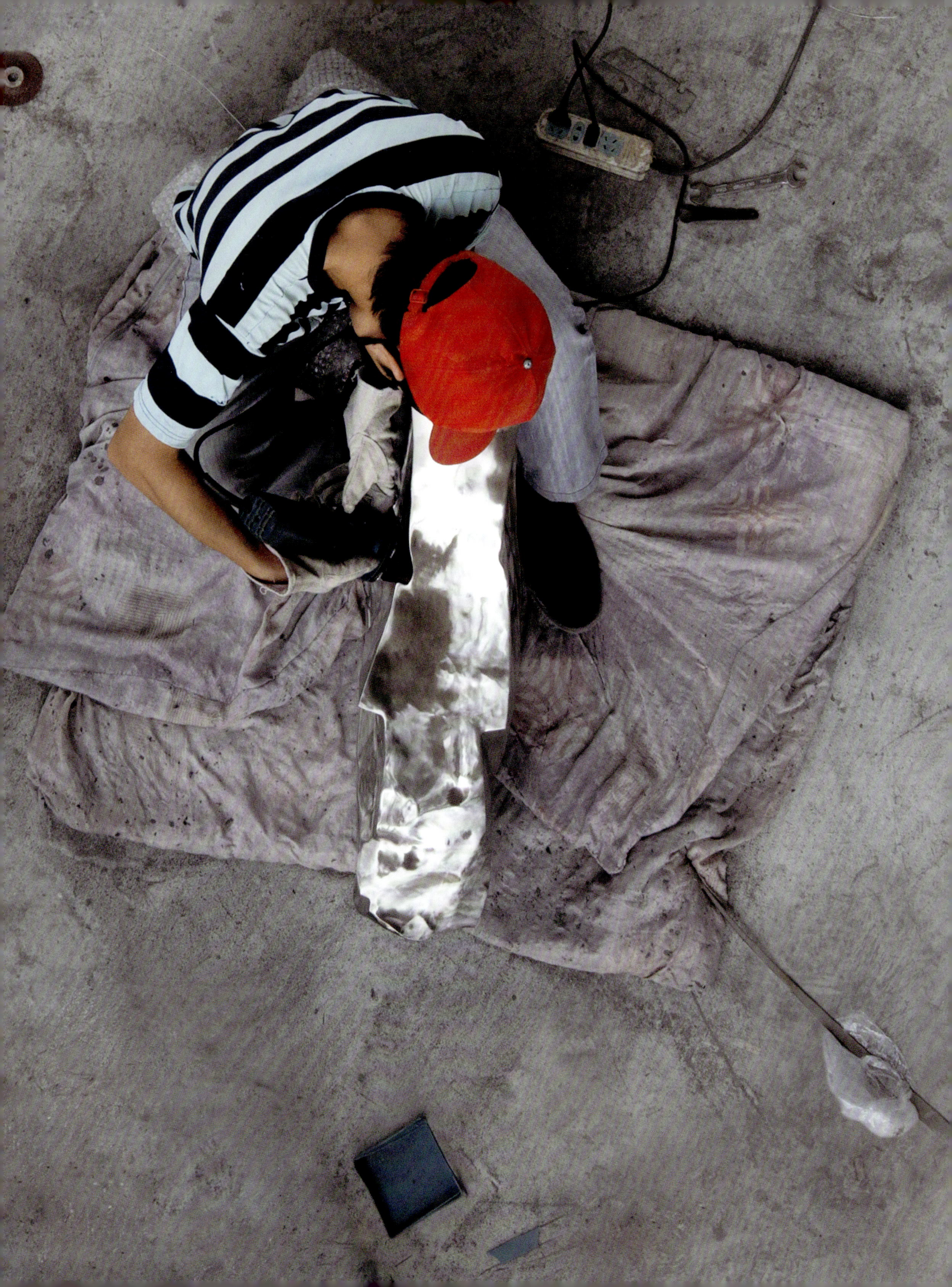

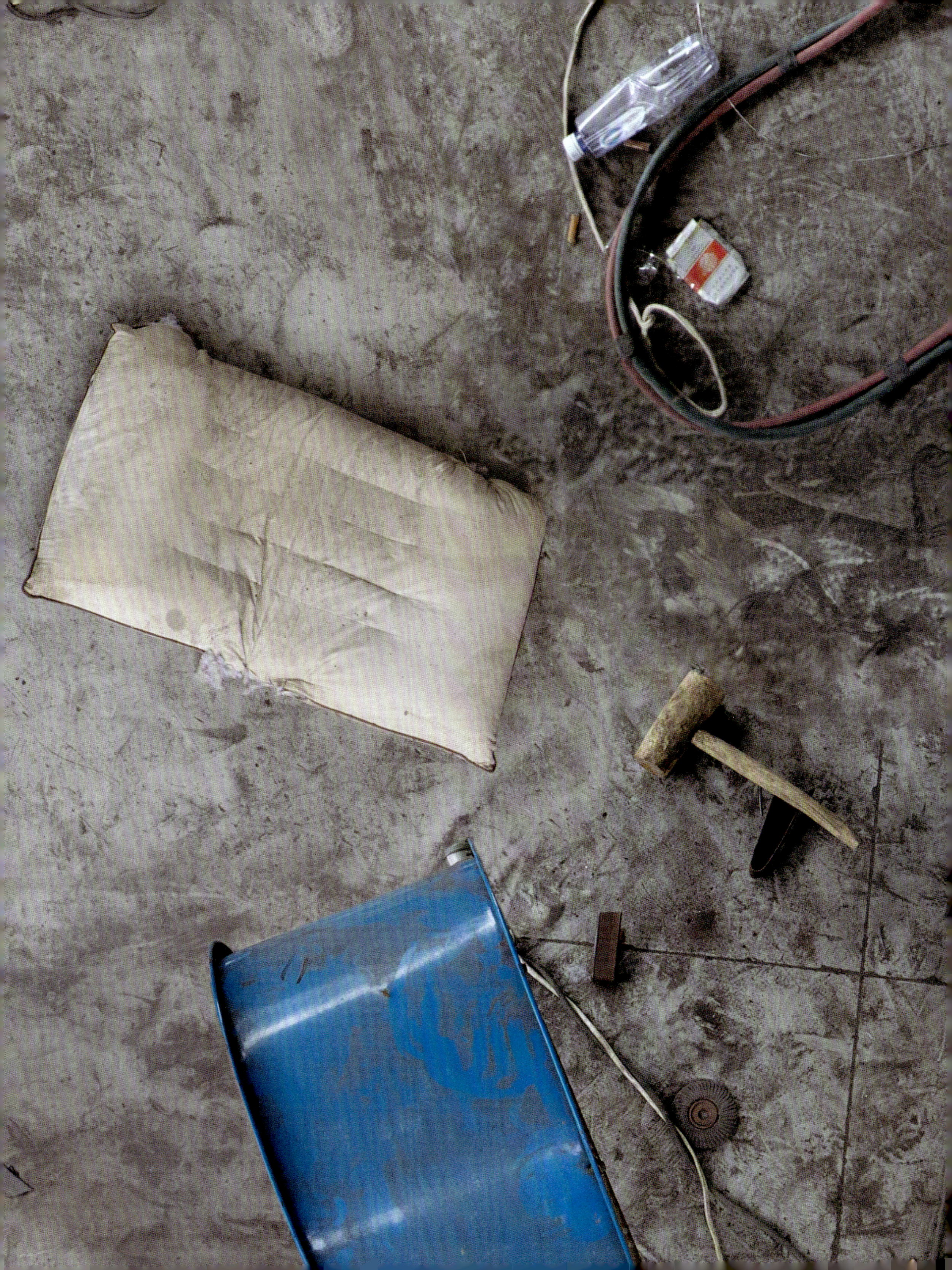

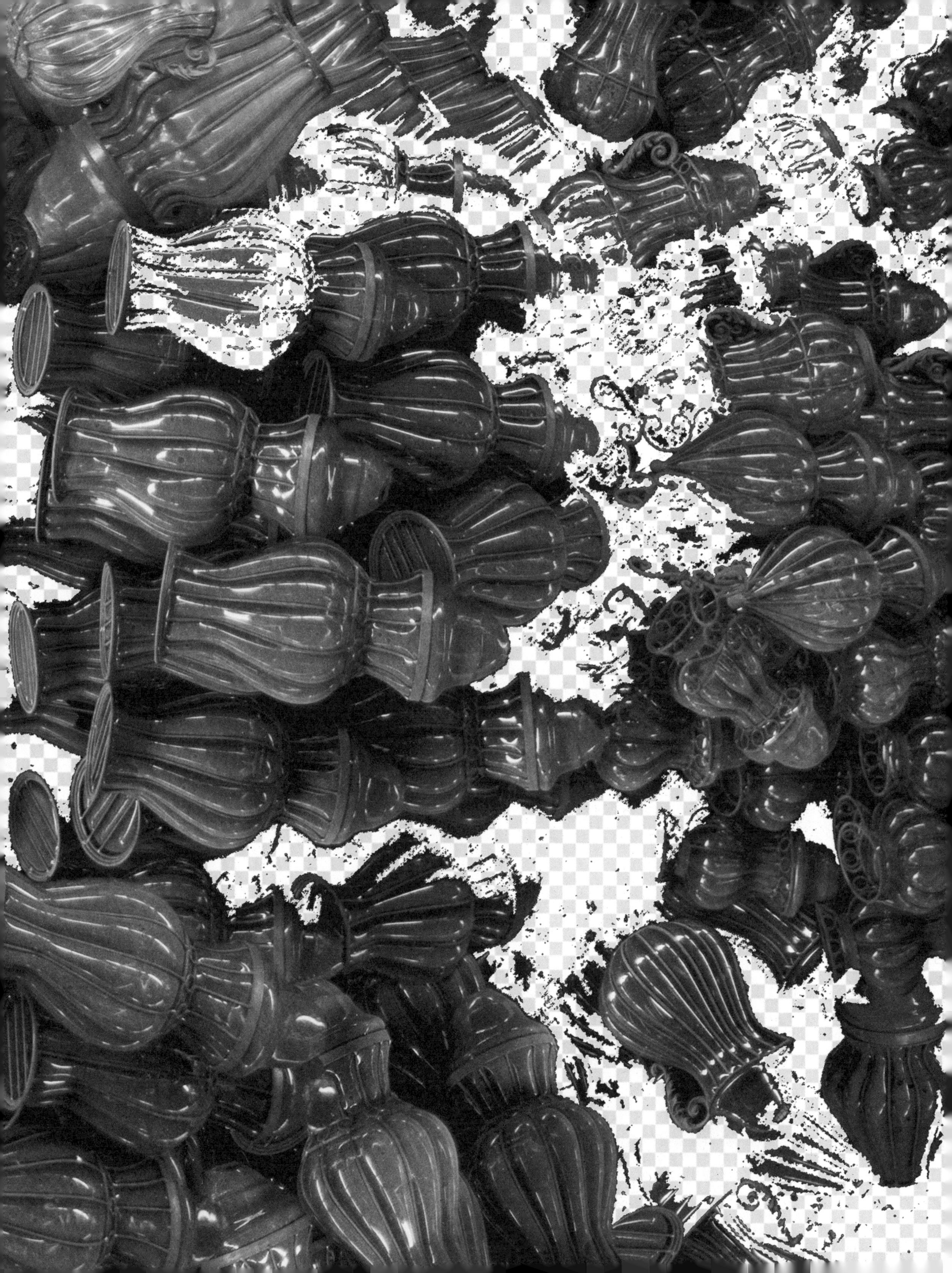

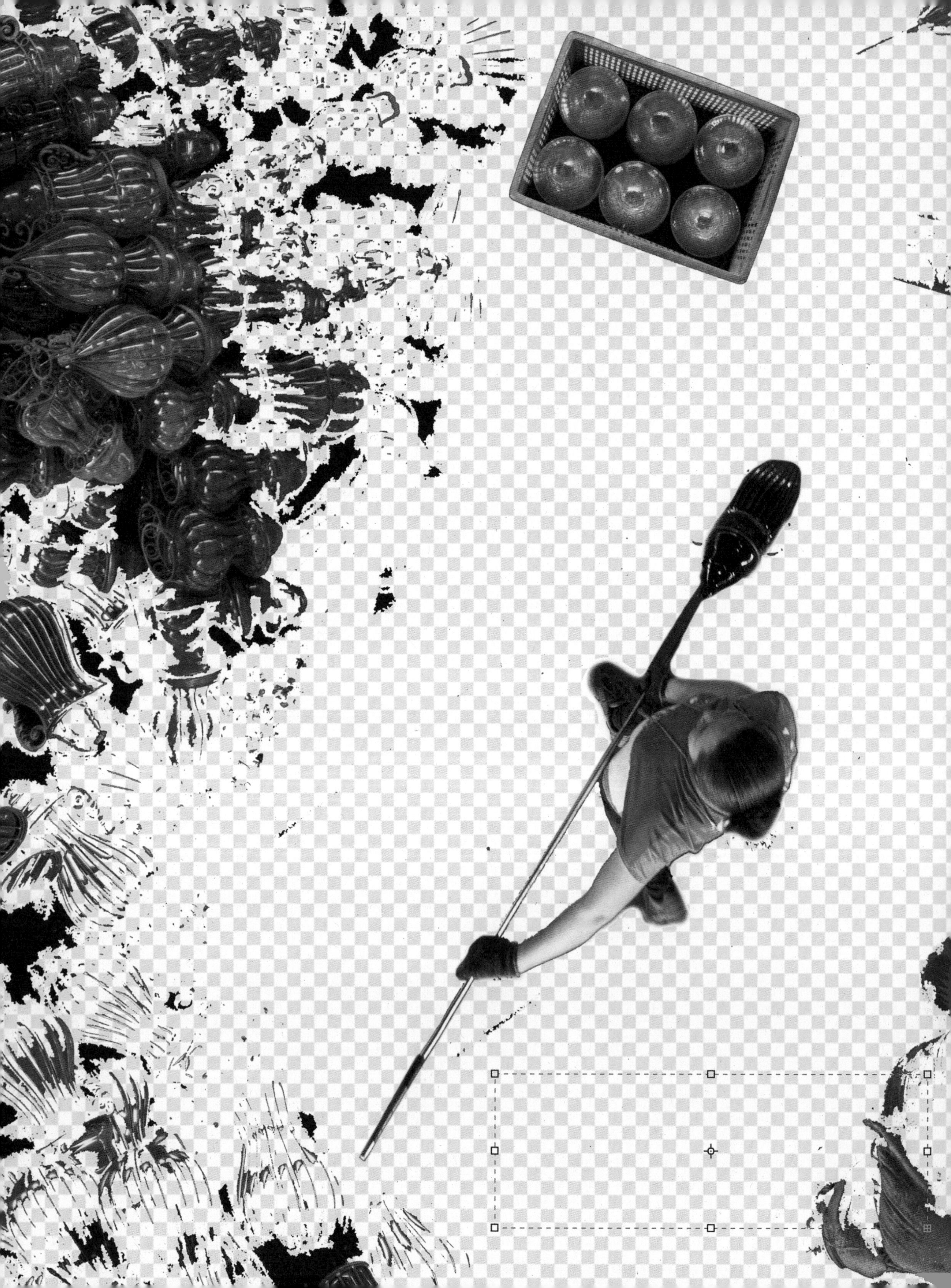

2.   No, Back Stages doesn't paint a picture of utopian labour conditions or ideal labour. The dust is far too visible, the noise is turned up too loud, the tools and the debris are scattered across the floor too carelessly, the kilns are too near and too hot. Certainly at the Chinese sites.
That doesn't mean the compositions would be void of societal comments.

At a closer look it becomes clear that Back Stages refrains from the political-cultural wars, waged all over the world for two decennia now, that are characterised by an anger that seems to be growing darker every day.

The current society seems to be coming apart at the seams. Consensus is crumbling, on any conceivable issue. Migration, distribution of wealth, the weather, god, the water, the arts, biodiversity, God, Black Peter and Saint Nicholas, democracy, museums, the neighbour's dress, enlightened despotism, dark despotism, lust, feminism, love, masculinity, modernism, obscurantism. Yeats is being dusted off: 'things fall apart. The centre cannot hold'.

Polarisation and fragmentation lead to cynicism in the cultural elite, an impossibility to see a brighter future, an inability to imagine a social alternative beyond the tendency to hold on even tighter to established privileges. In the margins, subcultures are roaming about, entangled in a contest of radicalisms and extremisms.
In a frontal assault on the Enlightenment's assumption of equality, for instance, or in a docile submission to political, ecological, economical prerogatives. A call for immediate action and a conspicuous symbolism to improve the world in any direction whatsoever. For agitation and propaganda, really. For the production of lies.

That is not the feeling I get from Back Stages.

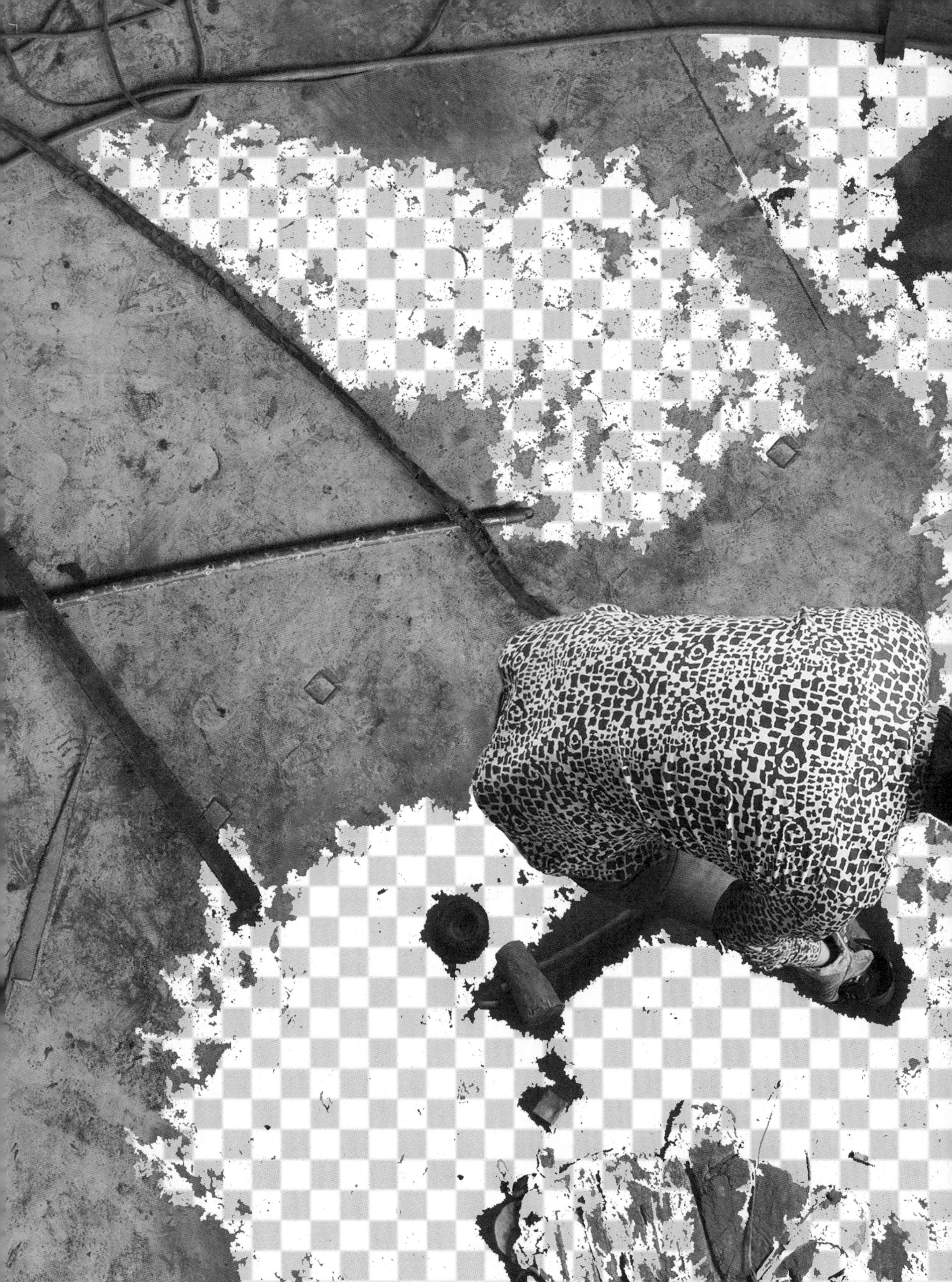

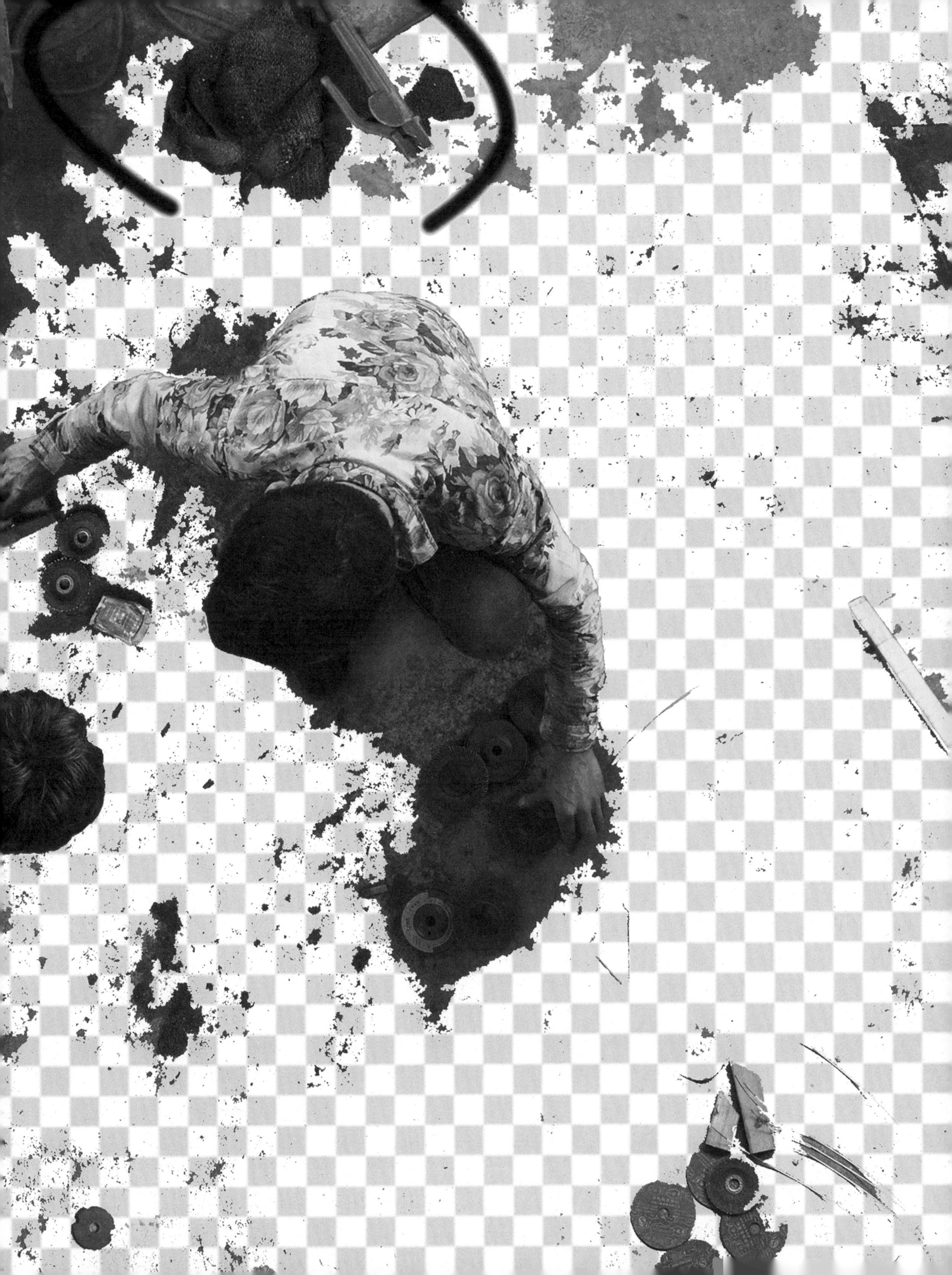

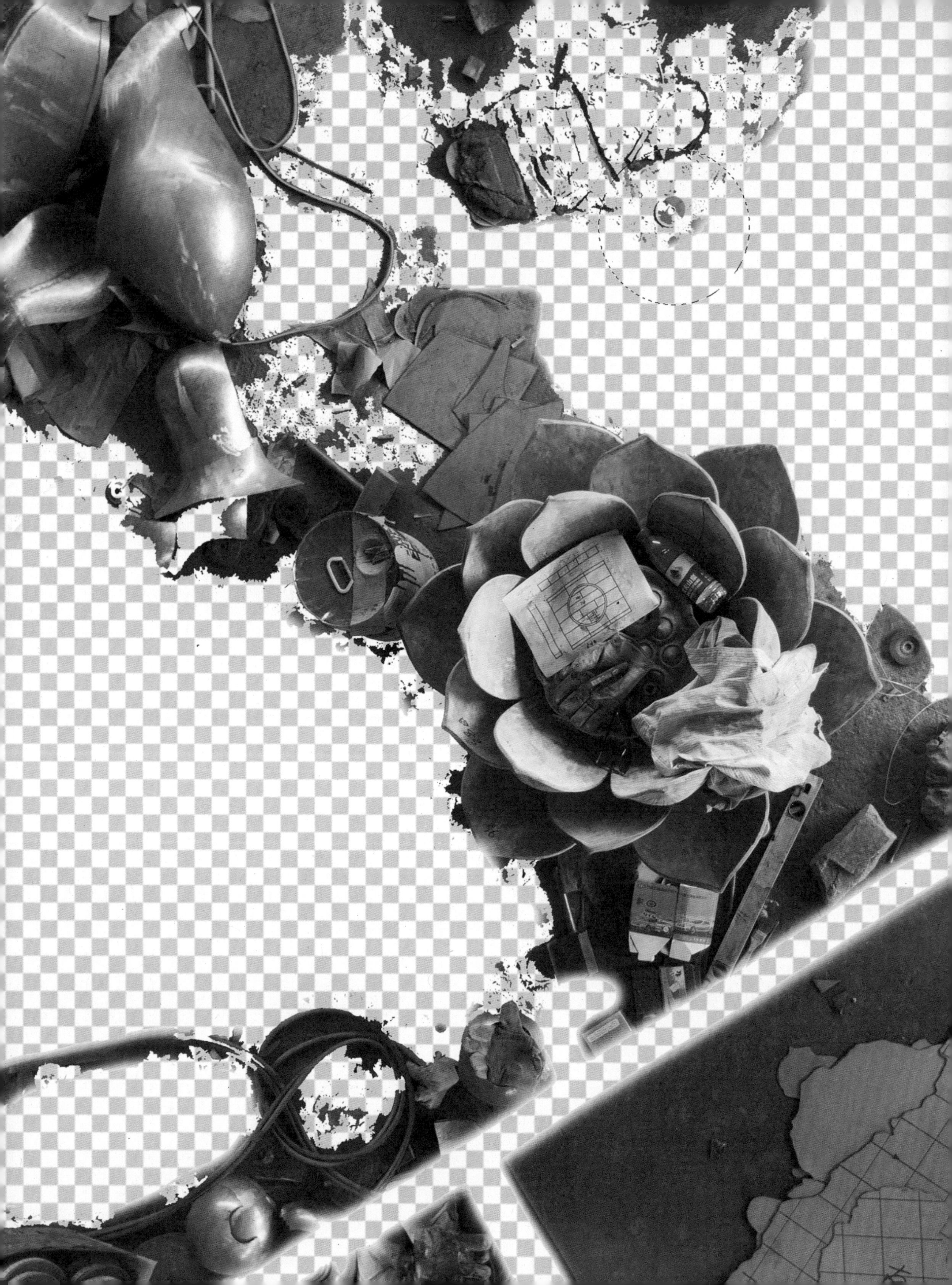

Back Stages evokes a societal space averse from cynicism, the smell of vomit, teargas and urine in the societal dead-end street, from aggressive populism and the fanatical belief in malleability and redemption.
A space founded on values of sharing, common ownership and social cooperation.

The shop floors composed in the photo-paintings reveal relation-ships between people, objects, materials and spaces that speak of a certain ease of cooperation. That show mutual trust and, above all, suggest the actual production of actual products, instead of soap bubbles. A Richard Sennett-like sense of craftmanship.

The work of Korfmann and Pfeifer opens a gate, it articulates a desire for common property and common activity. For common good. For labour that leads to solidarity. Where words like home and homemade come together. Where a small, intimate choreography emerges from the common work process.

In their project, Korfmann and Pfeifer leave behind all the cynicism, the extremism and the incorporeality of contemporary cultural labour and art. It's not necessarily a conscious act of defiance, before anything it is an artistic gesture. It is a dream deed that doesn't revolt but takes documentation as a point of departure to create imaginative impressions. It is fiction.

The project's title, Back Stages, refers to the theatre. The grand dream machine. It is a pertinent choice. In the theatre, the reality of acting and the theatre's architecture converge with free imagination. The same happens in the photo-compositions that make up this project. The artists are directors, developing an actual utopian visual experience from their observations of reality.

But what kind of directing tricks do Korfmann and Pfeifer actually use to take this often underpaid, extremely demanding, sometimes unhealthy labour and turn it into a platform of reflection on good labour? And why are they so interested in making photo-paintings of places of labour to begin with?

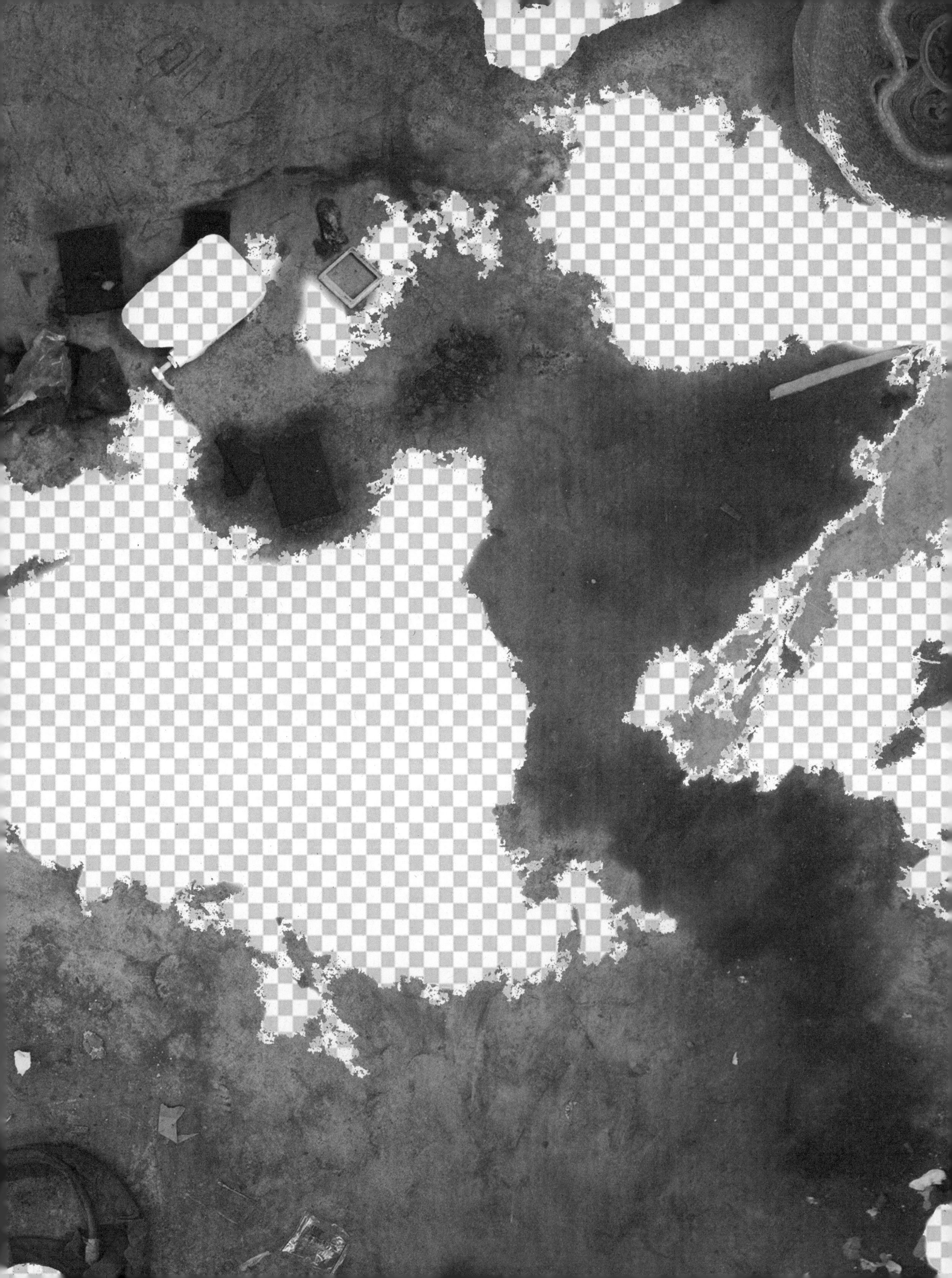

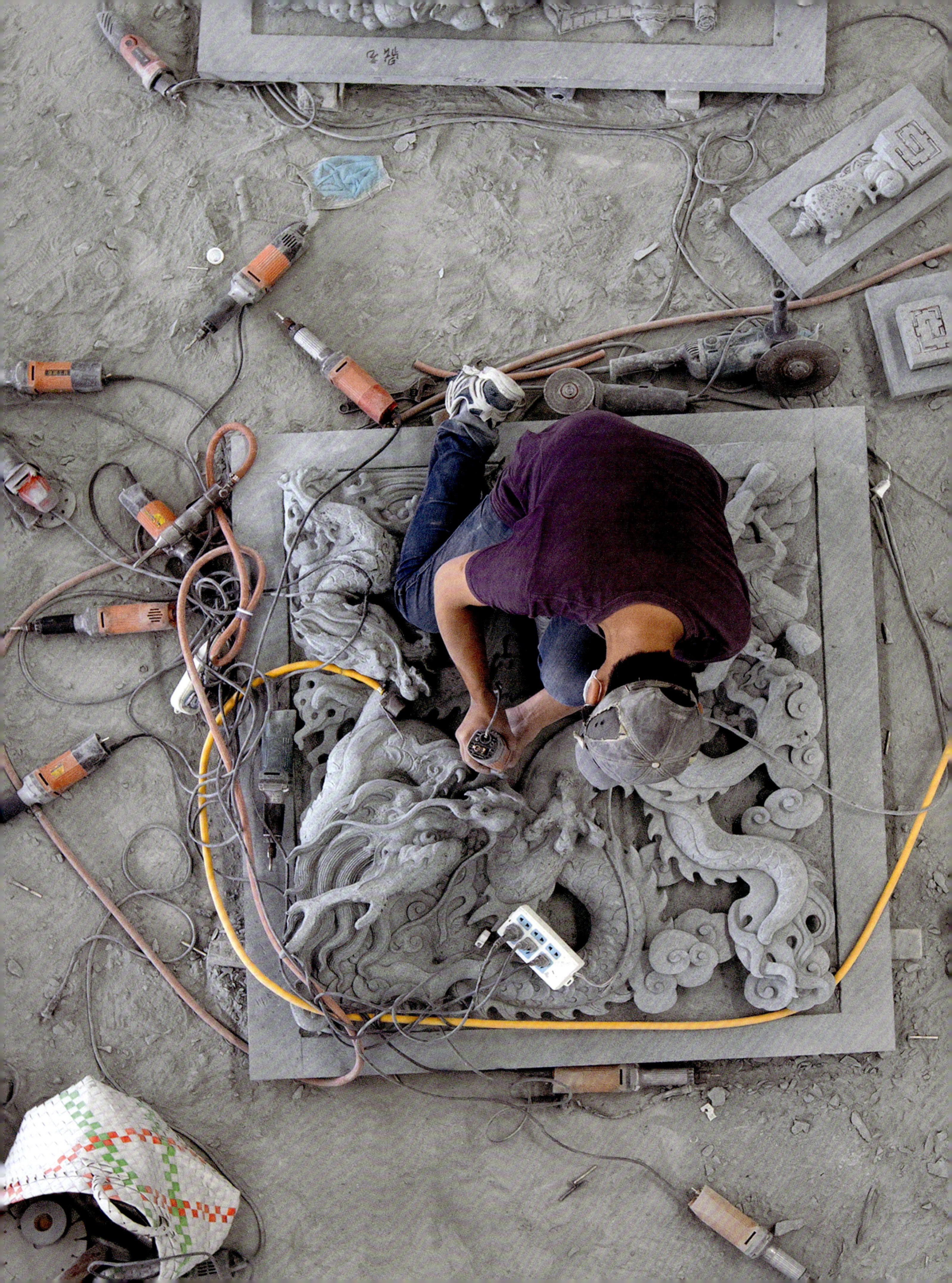

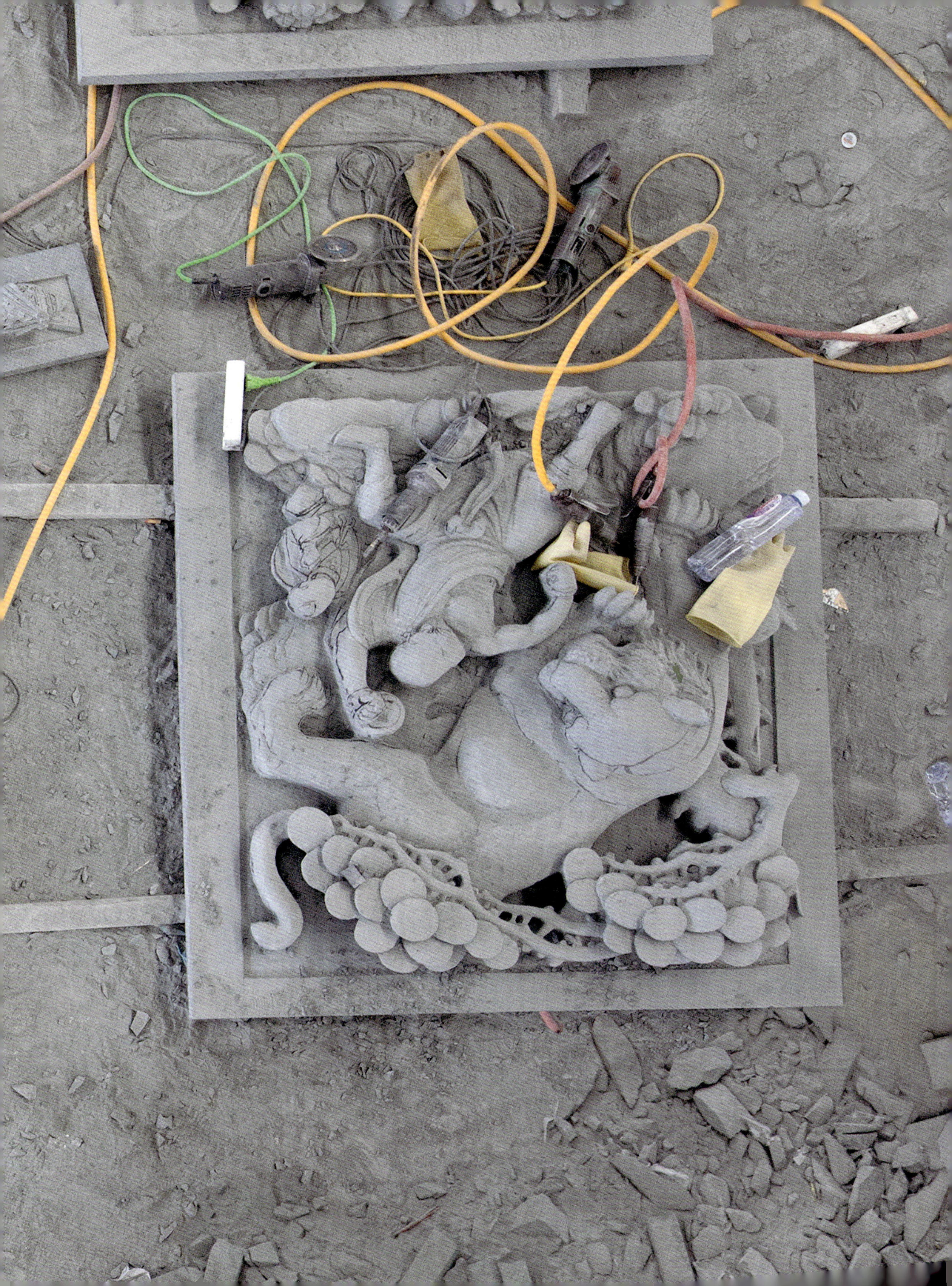

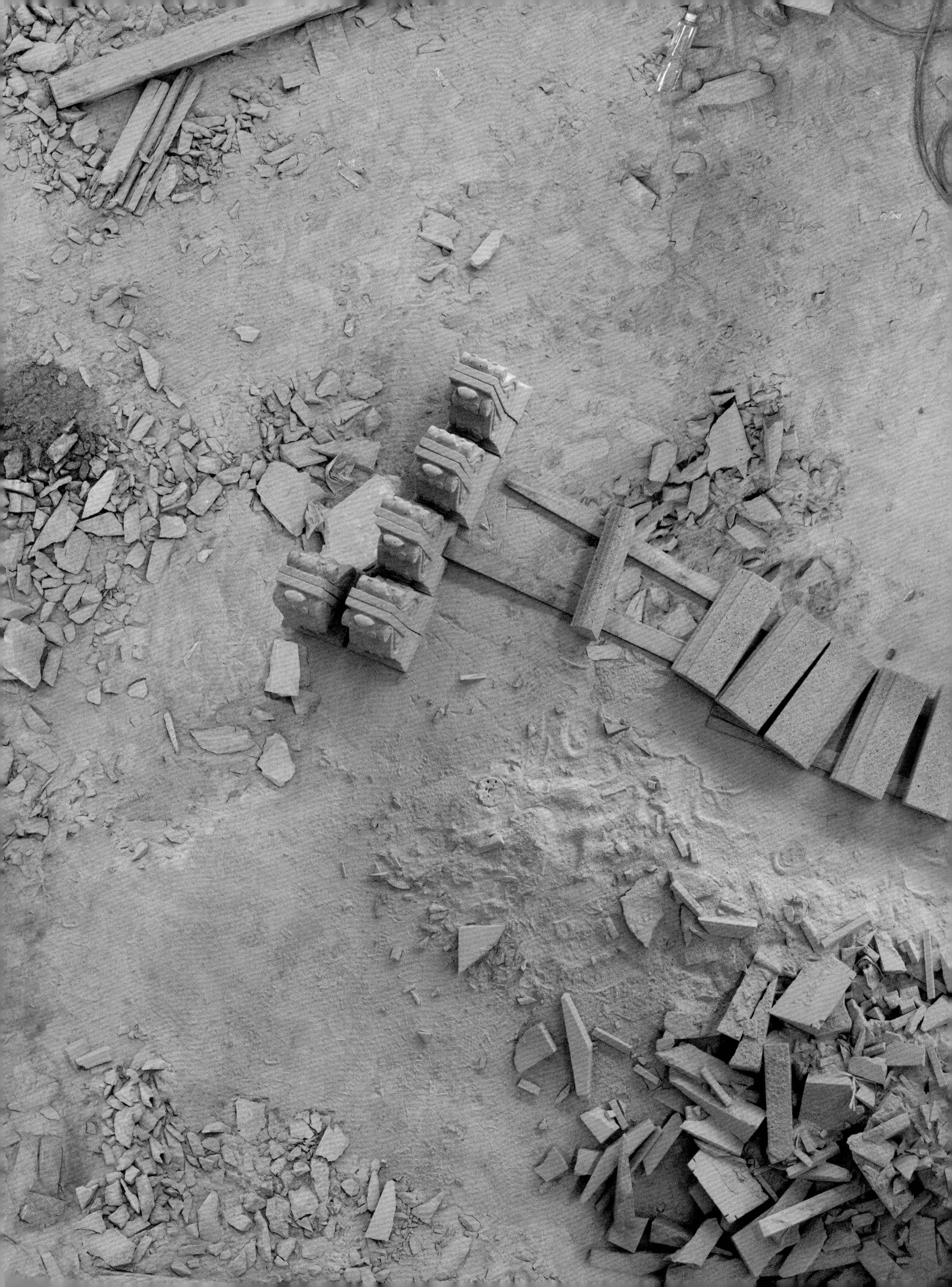

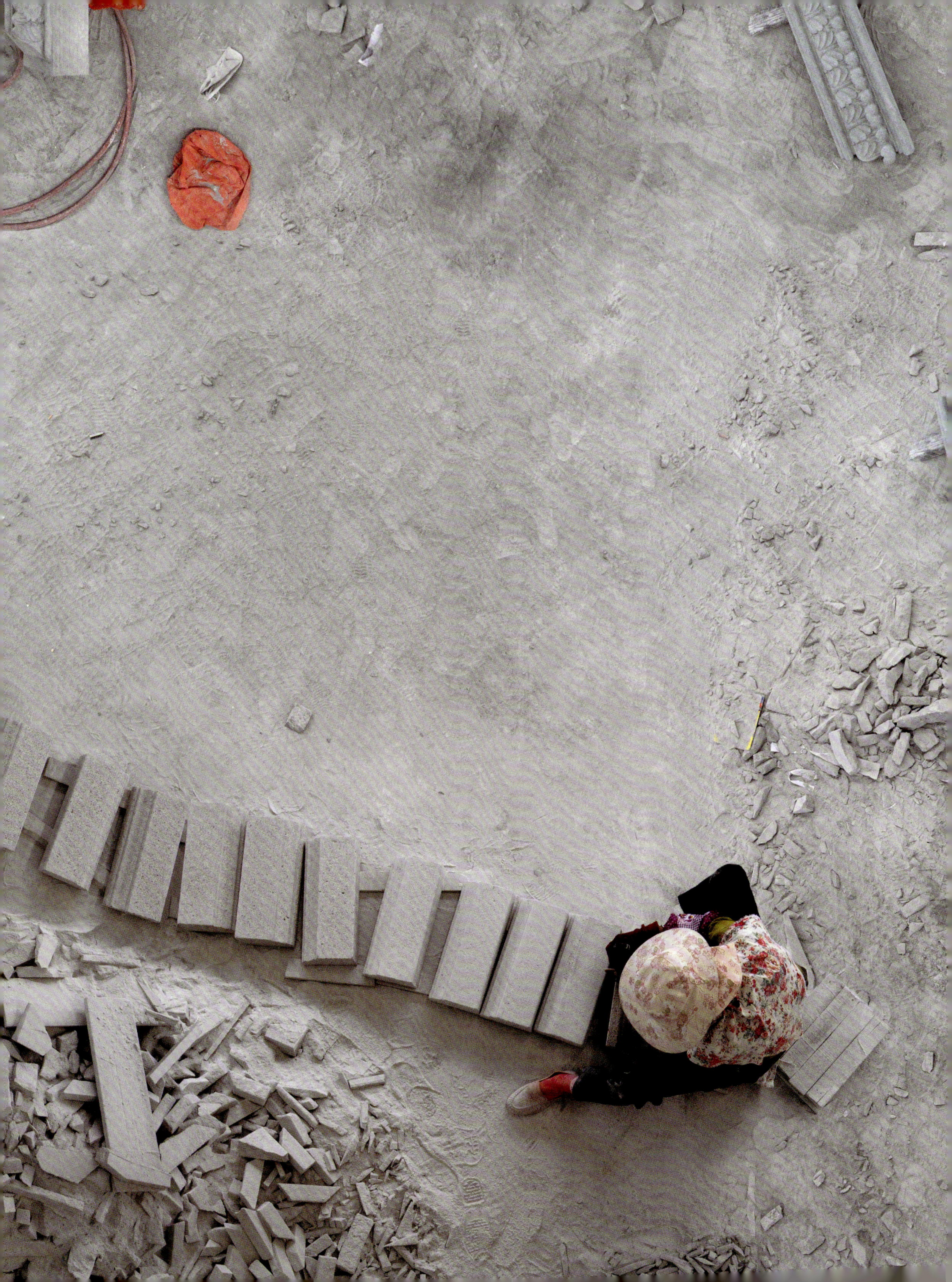

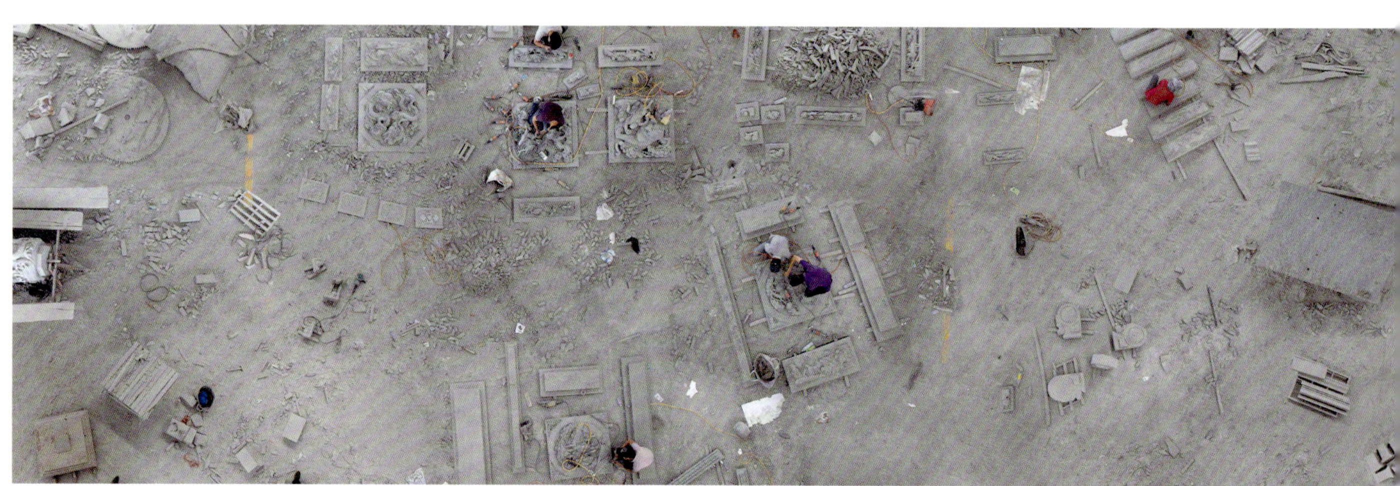

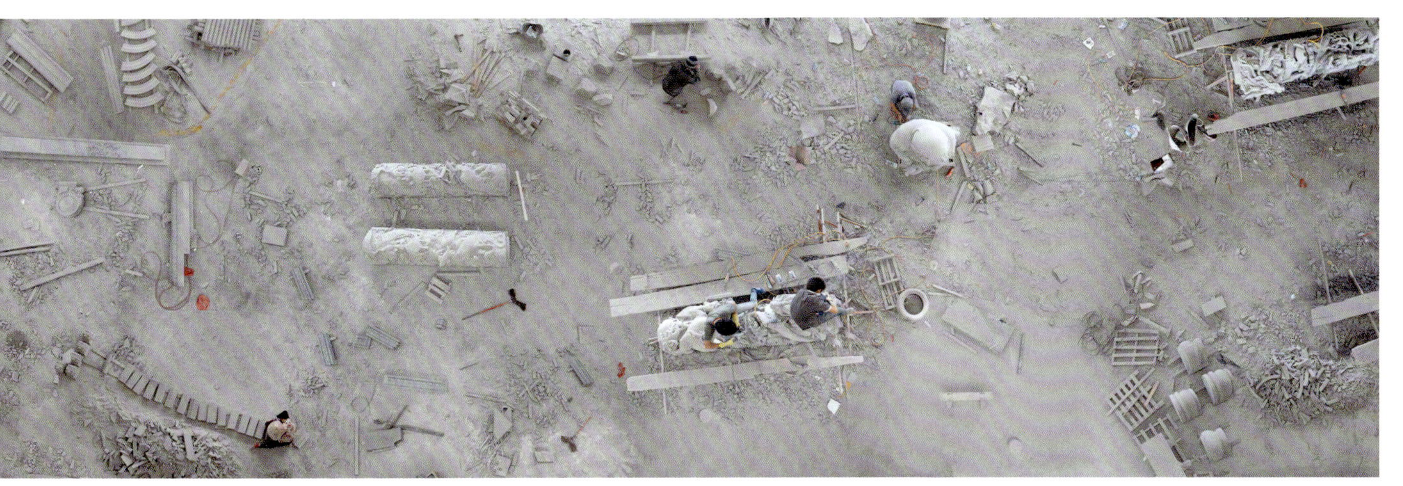

HUI'AN
Granite sculpture workshop in China
150 × 960 cm | 60" × 378" & 35 × 225 cm | 14" × 89"   59

TROY
Archaeological excavation in Troy, Turkey
350 × 243 cm | 138" × 96" & 173 × 120 cm | 68" × 47"

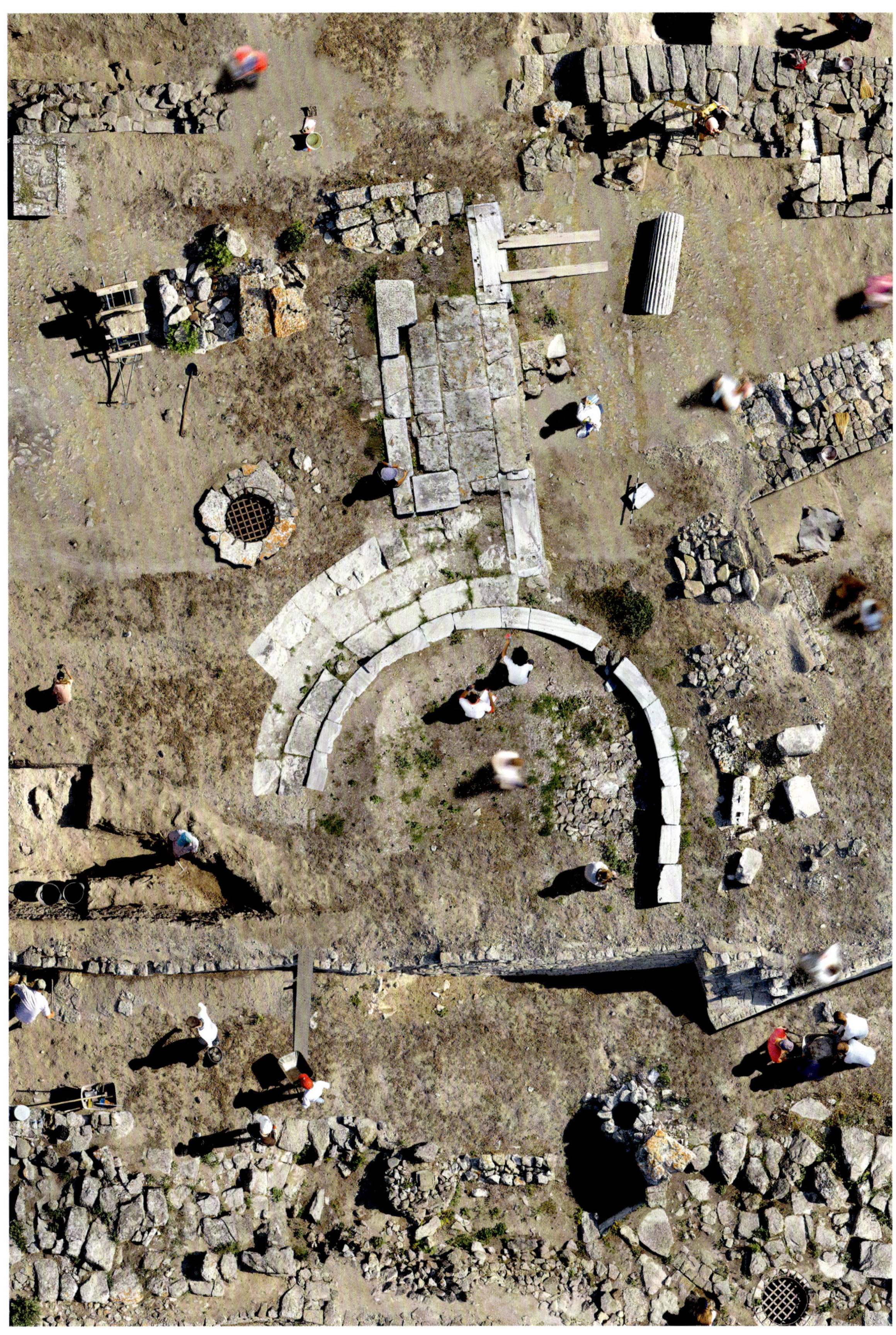

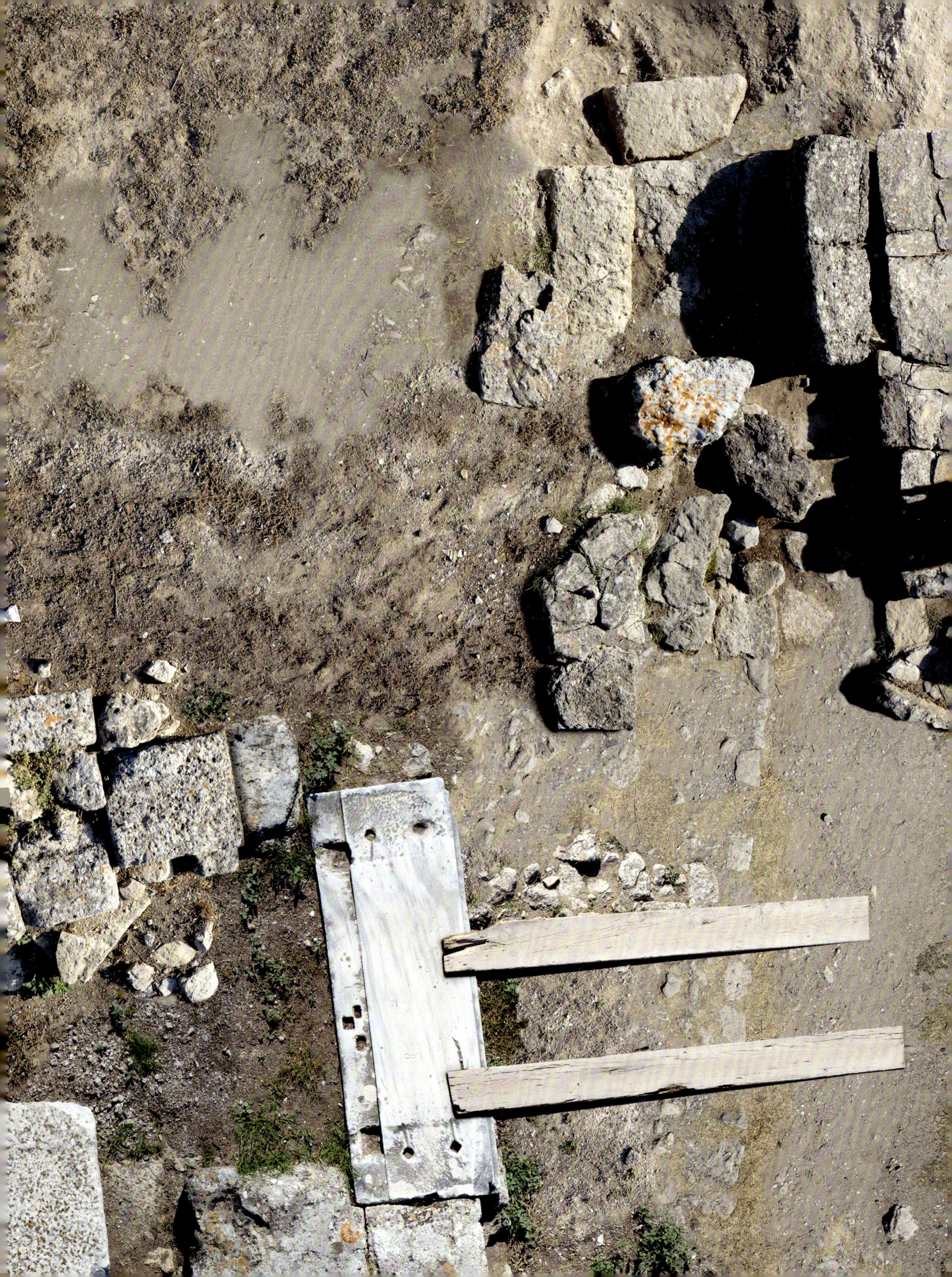

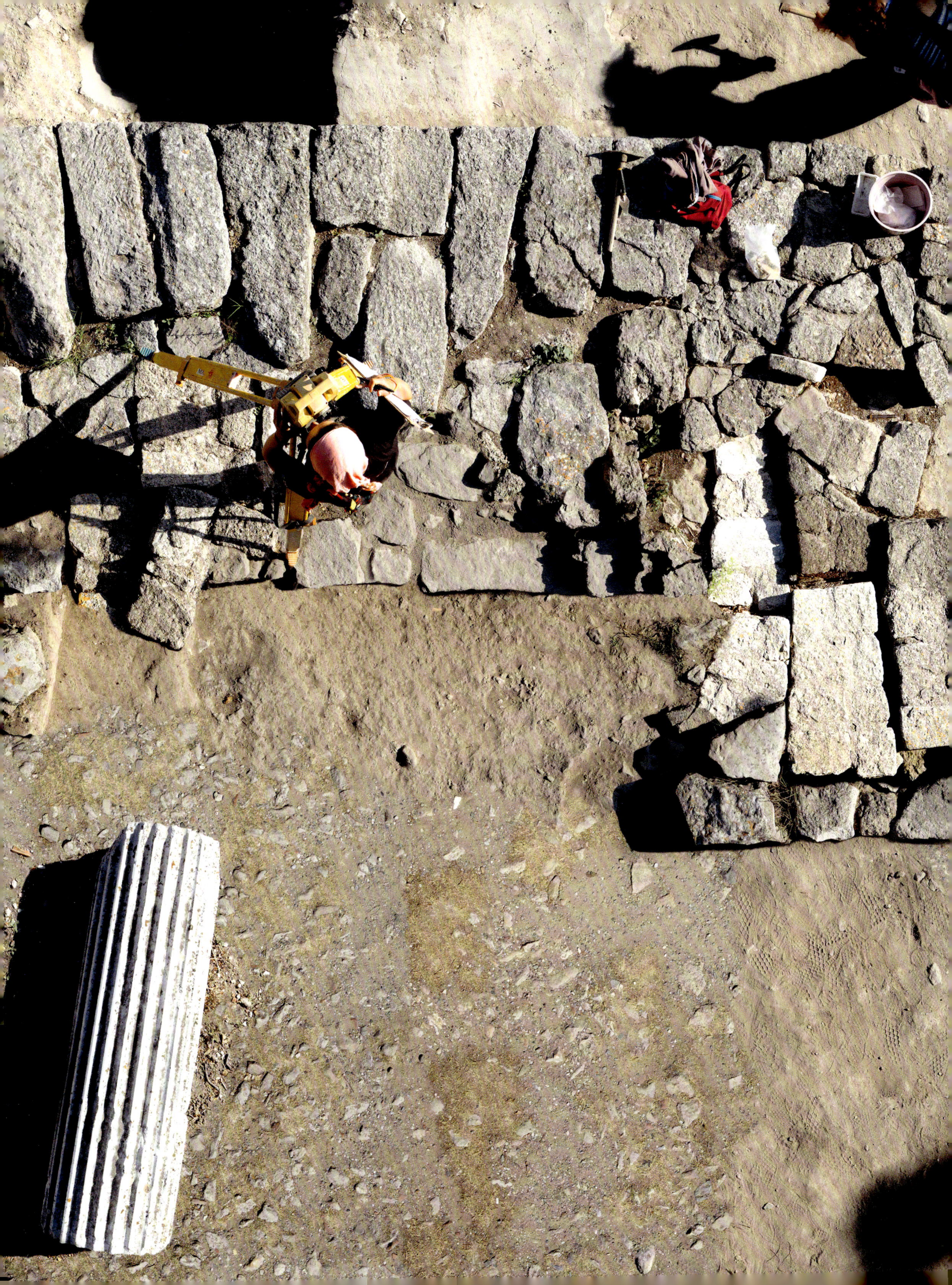

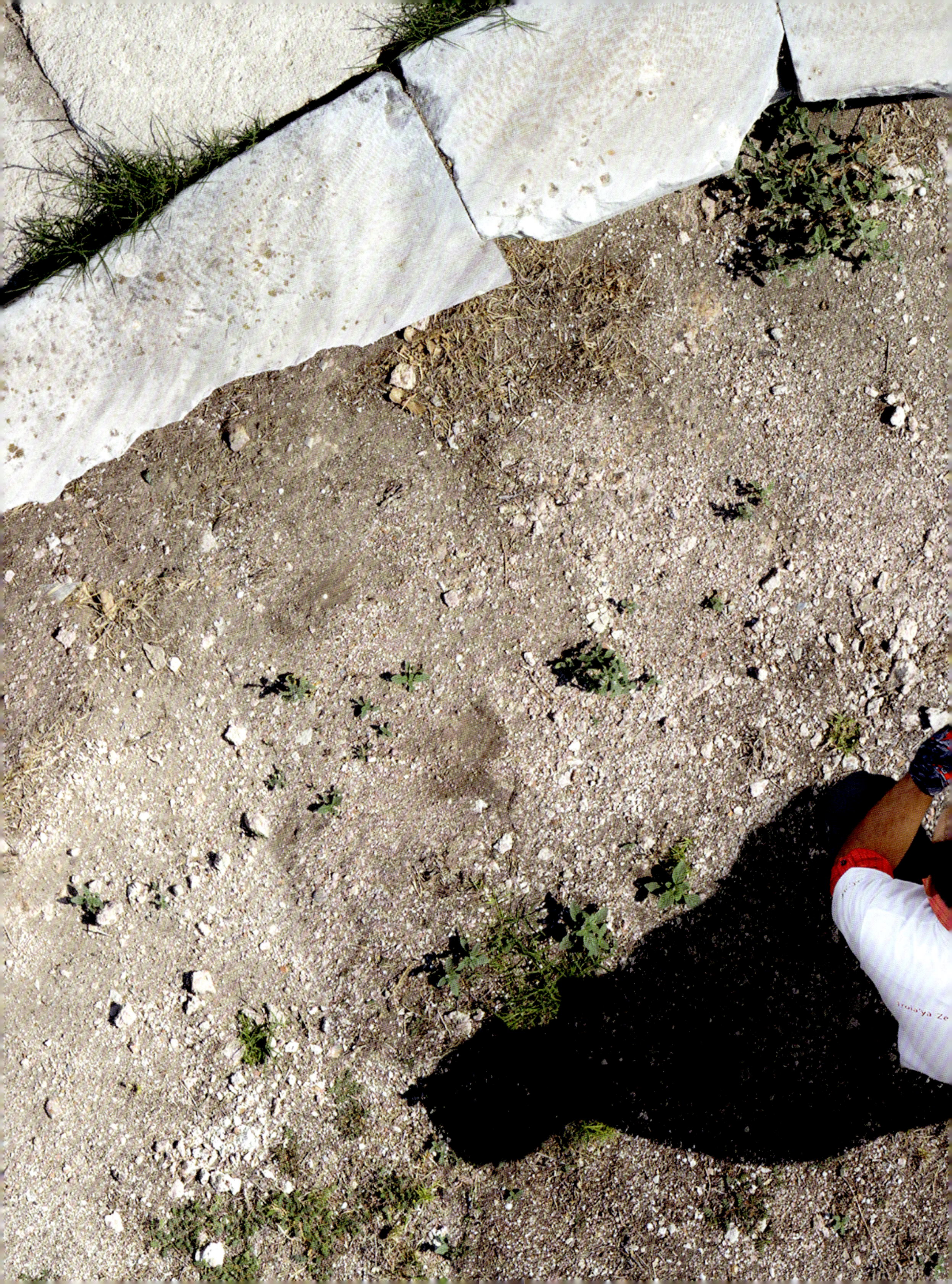

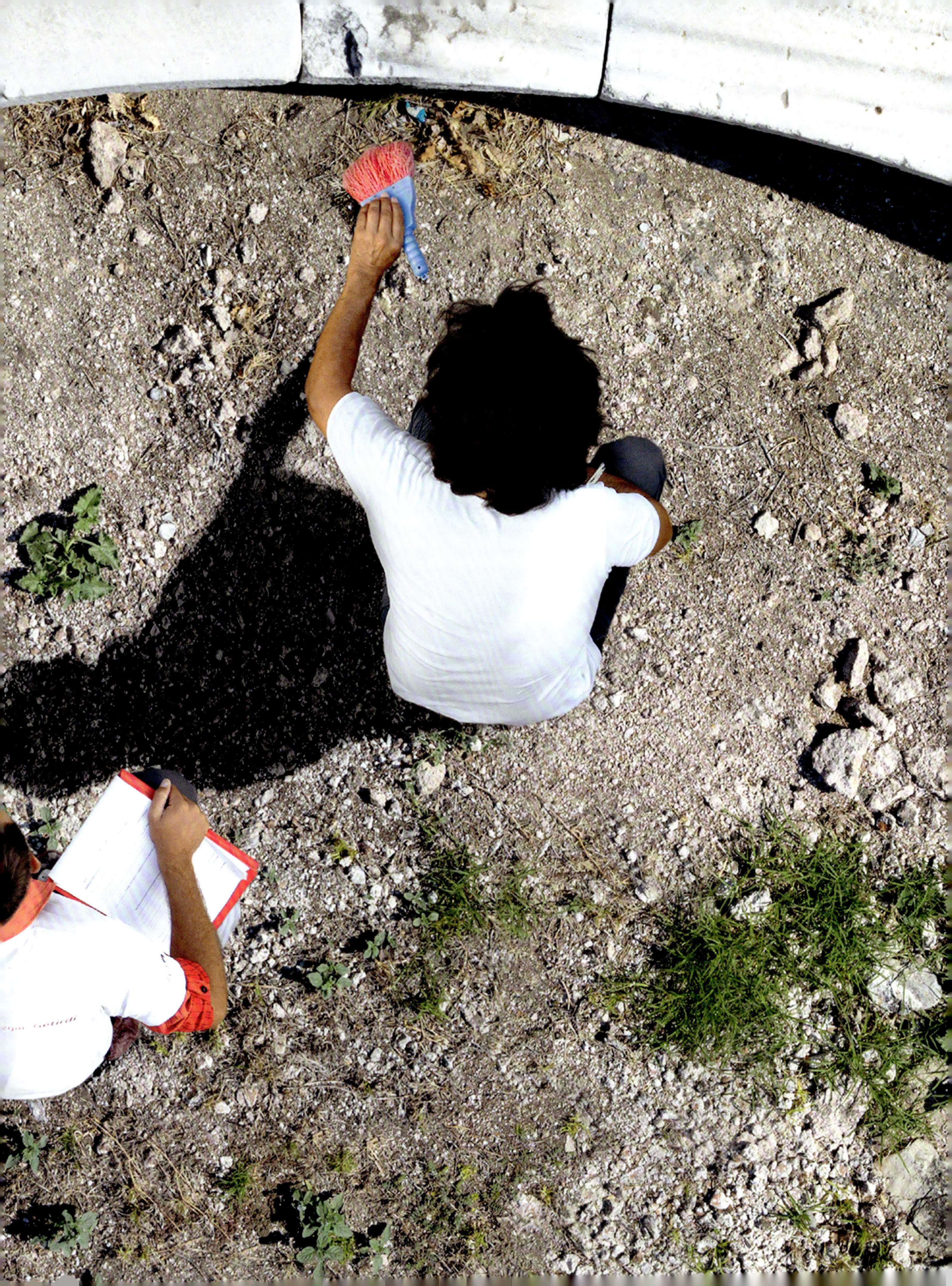

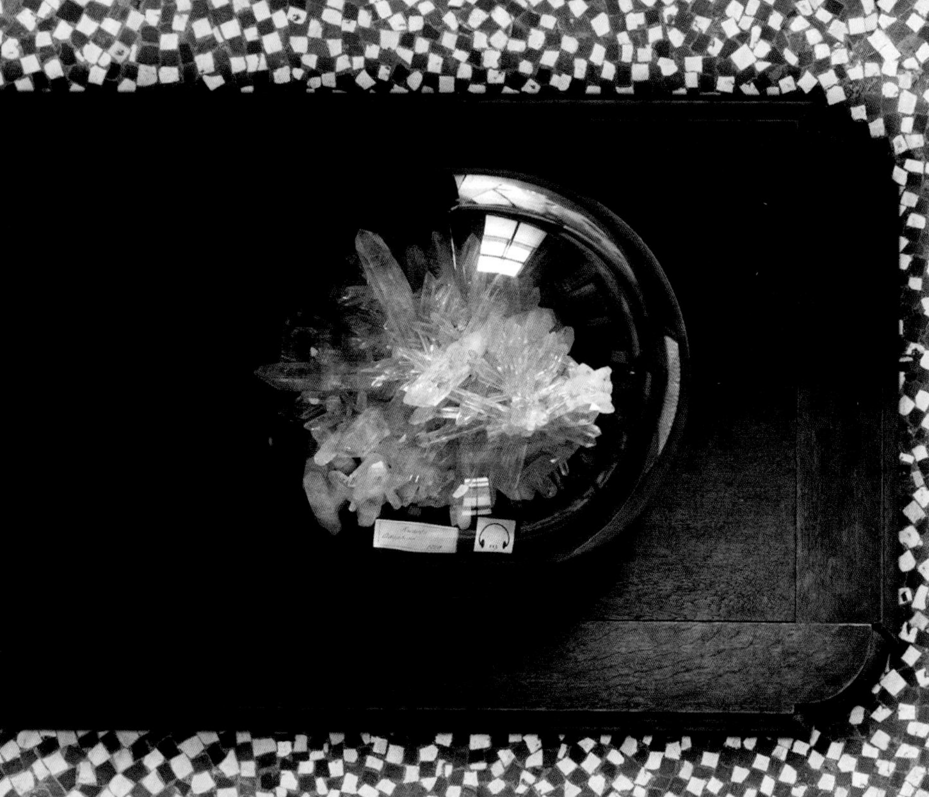
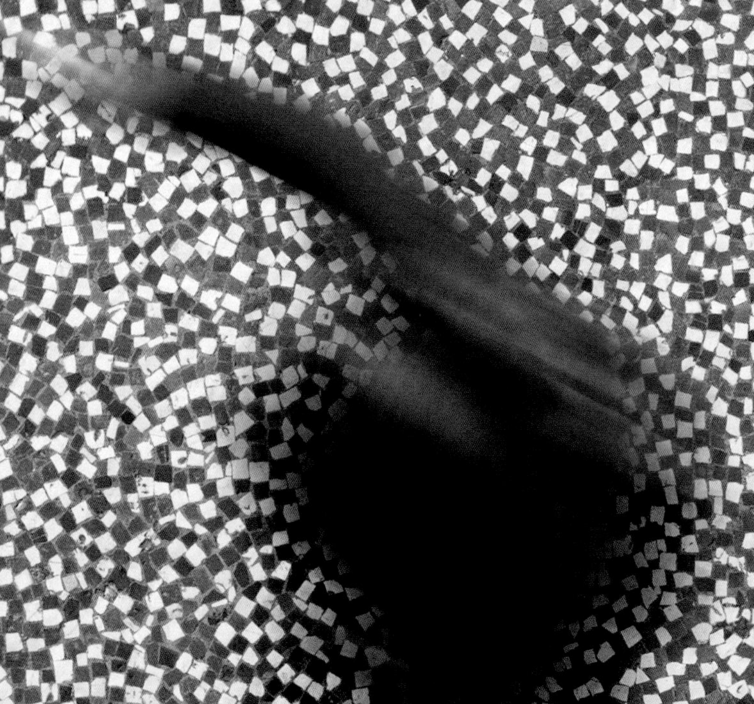
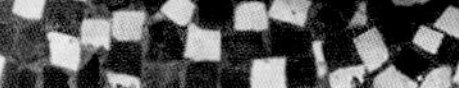
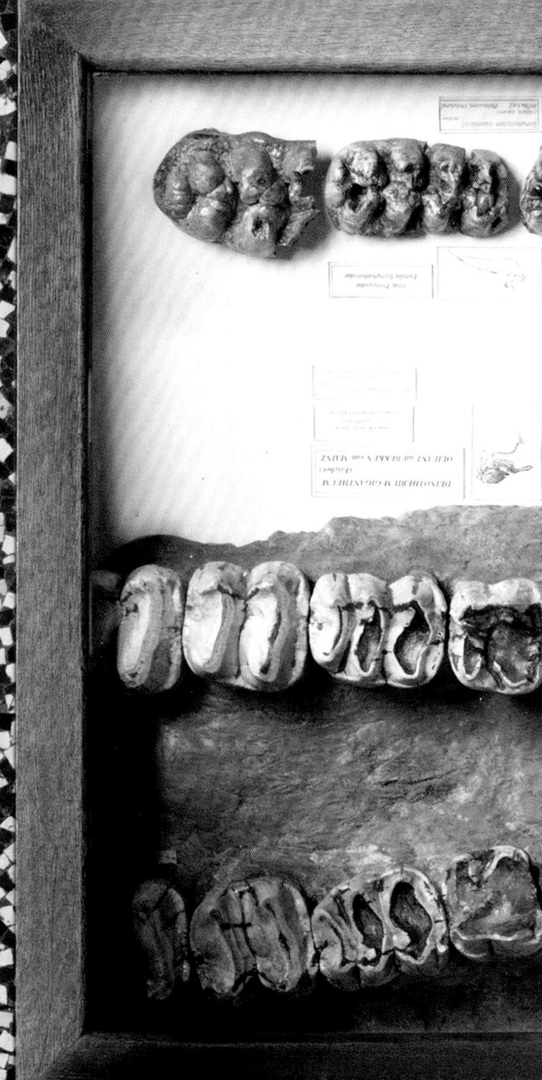

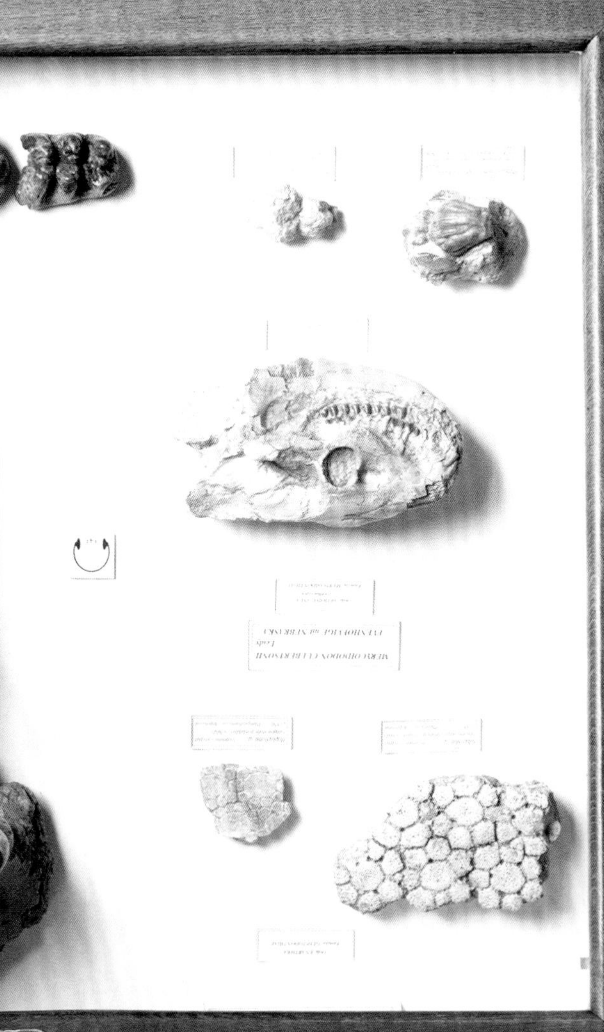
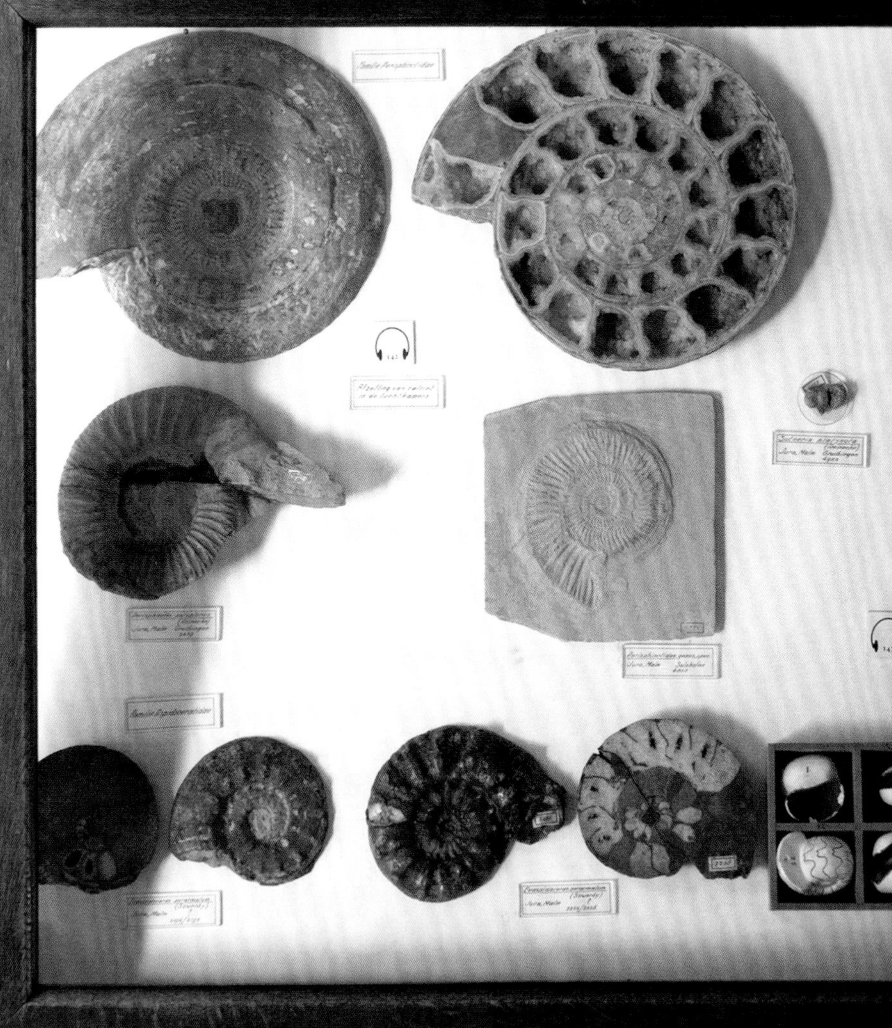

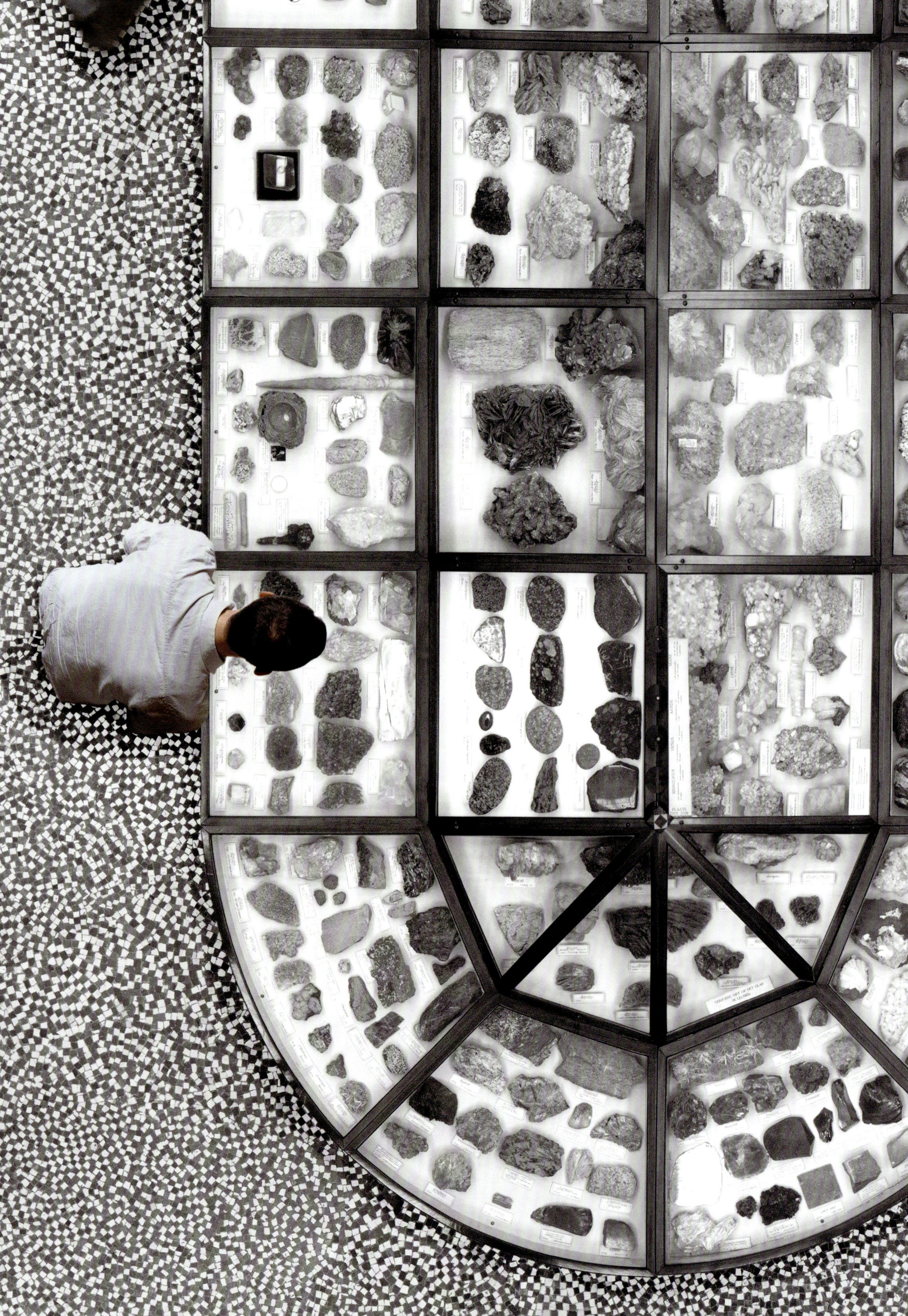

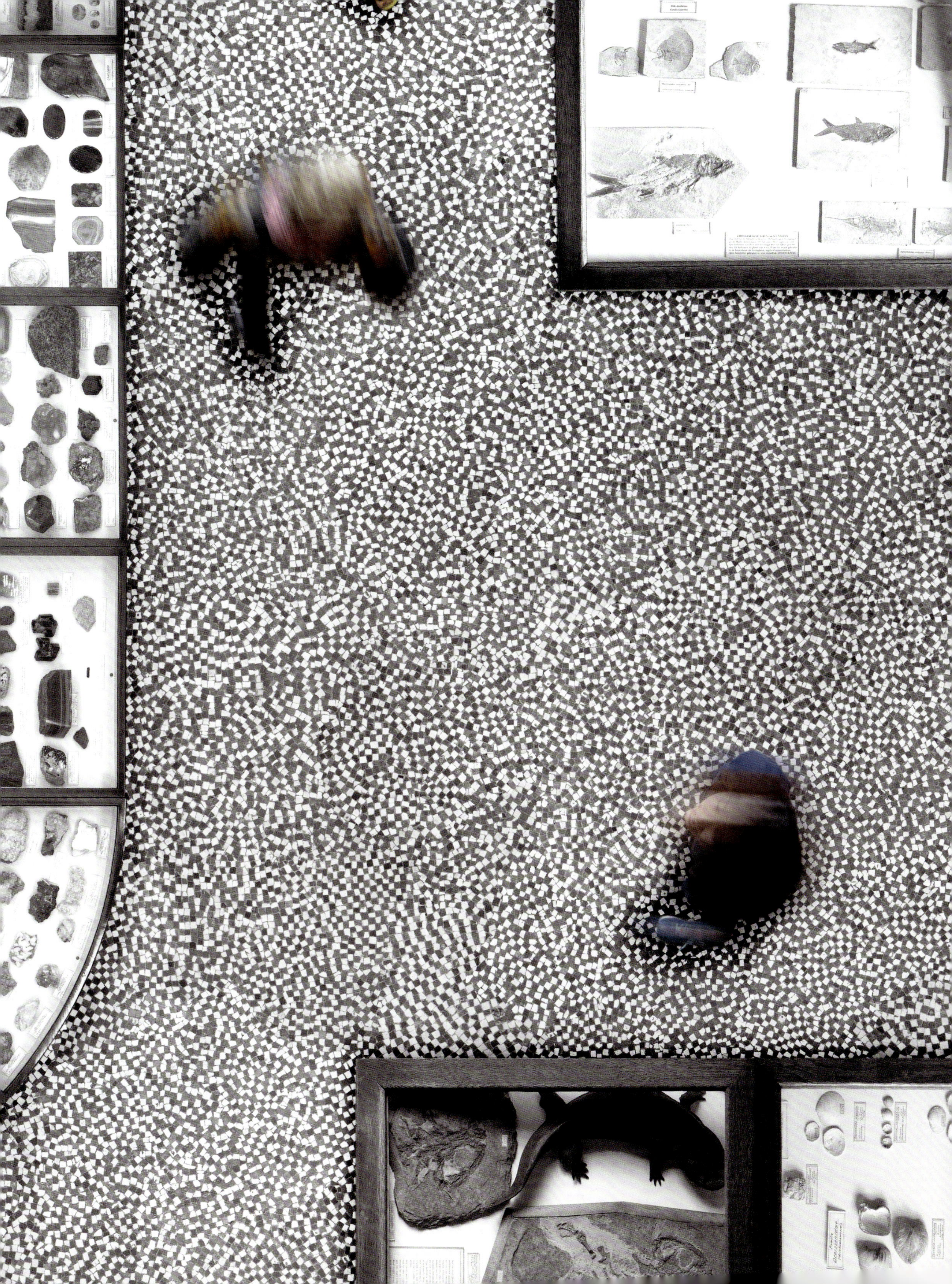

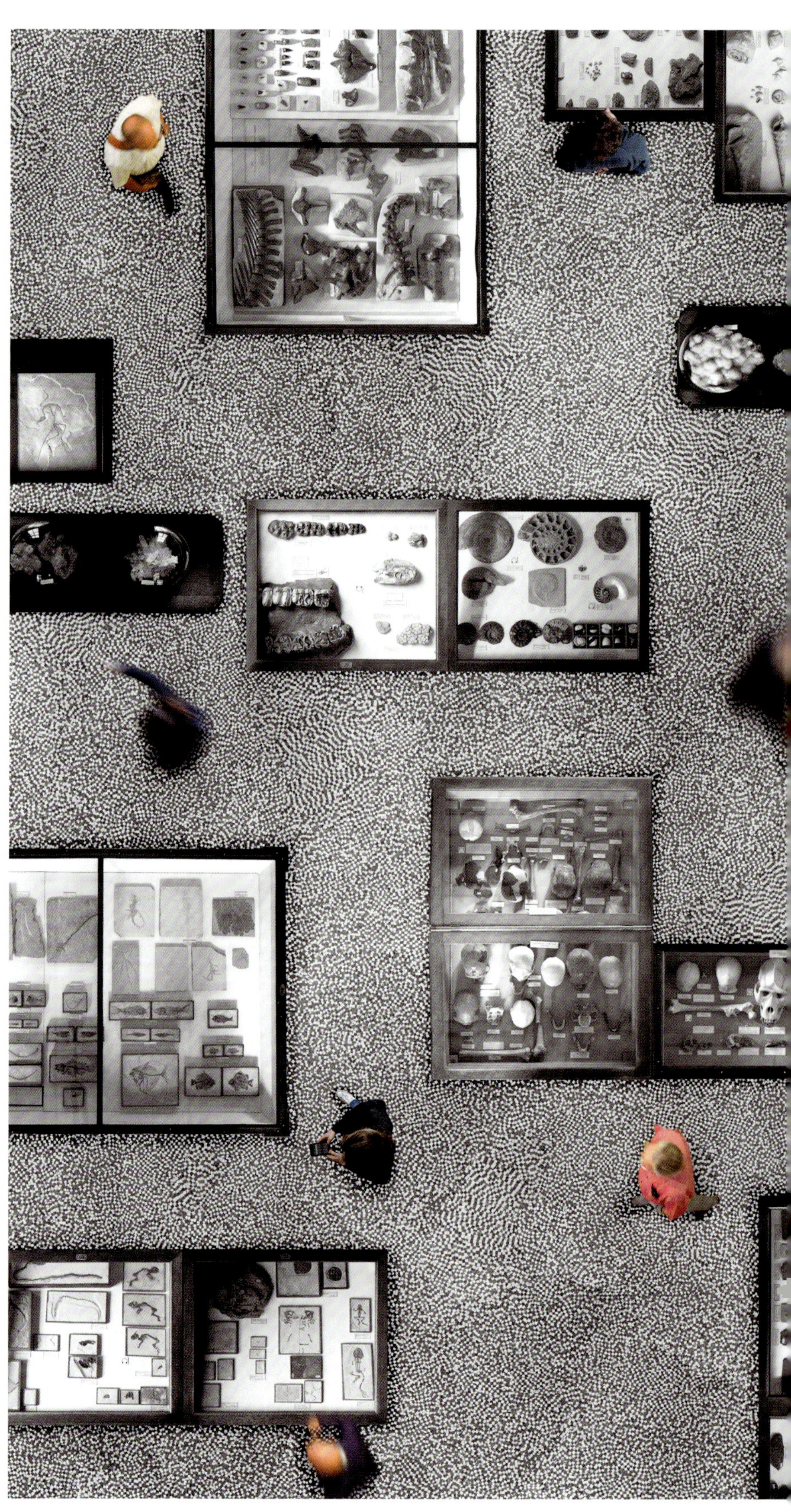

TEYLERS, HAARLEM
18th-century museum for the arts and sciences in the Netherlands
300 × 430 cm | 118" × 170" & 120 × 173 | 47" × 68"

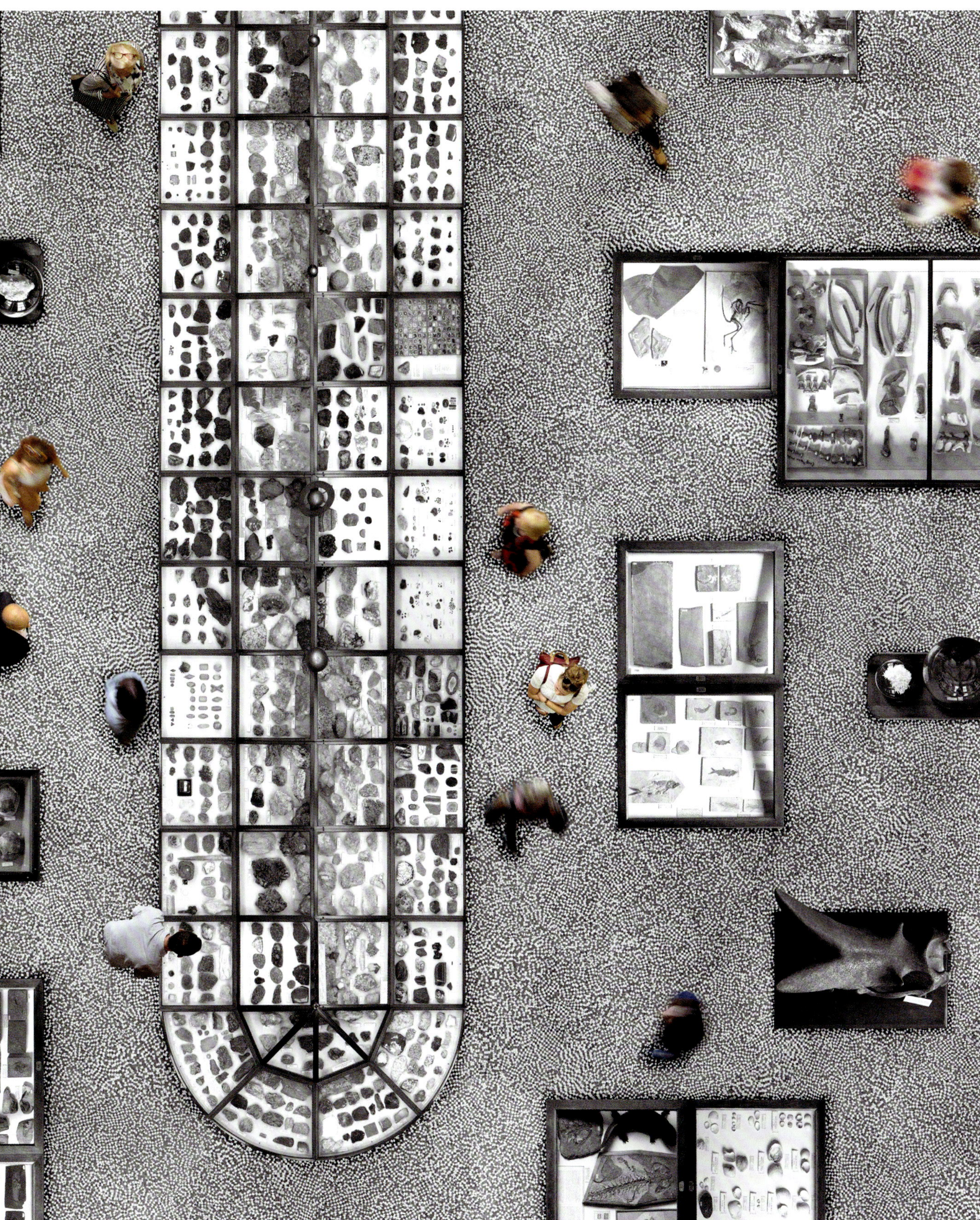

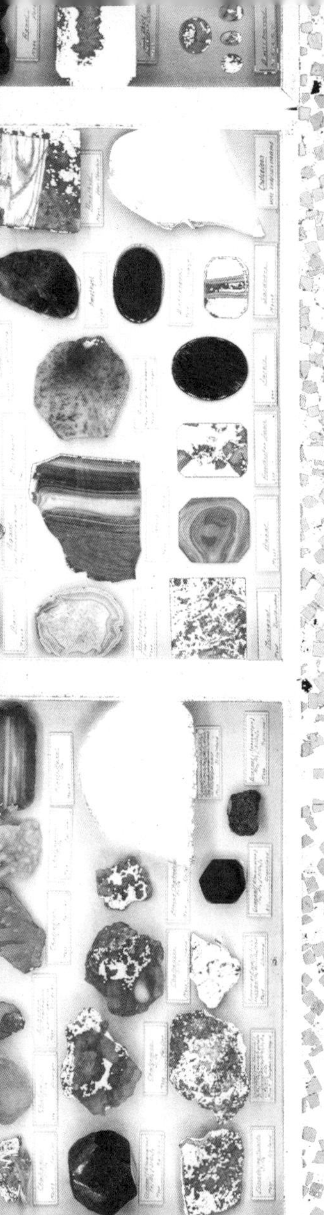
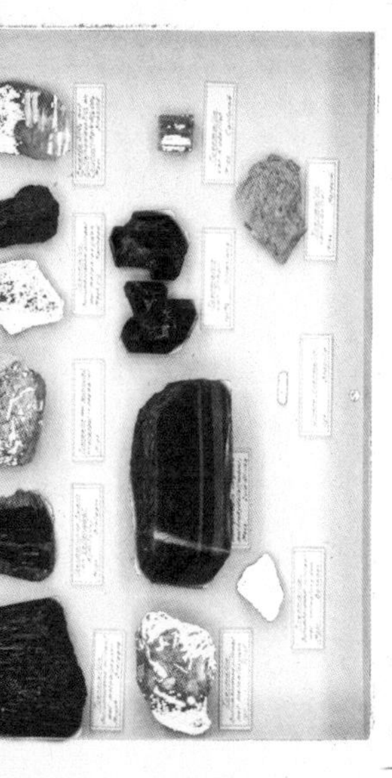
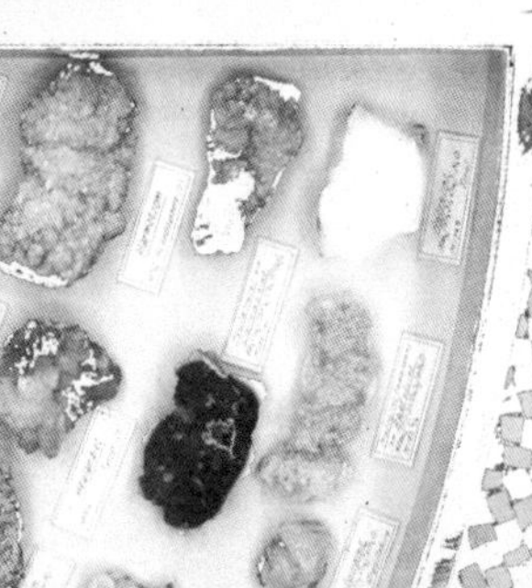
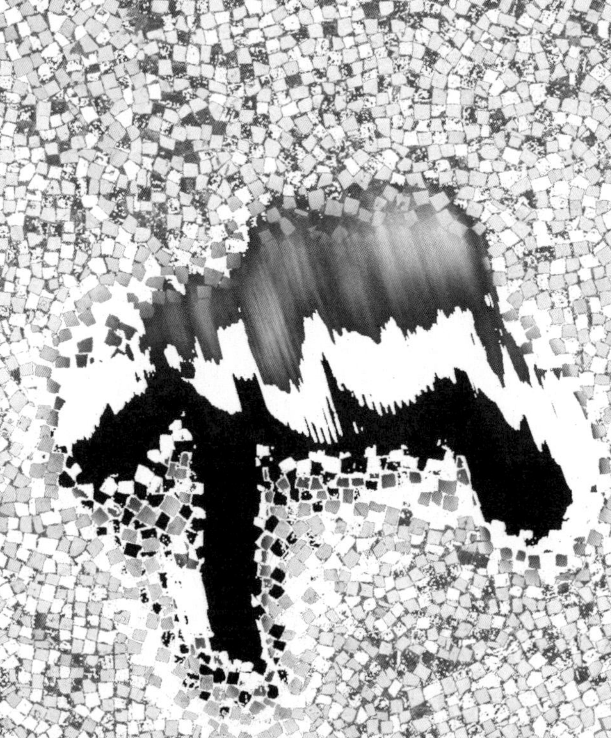

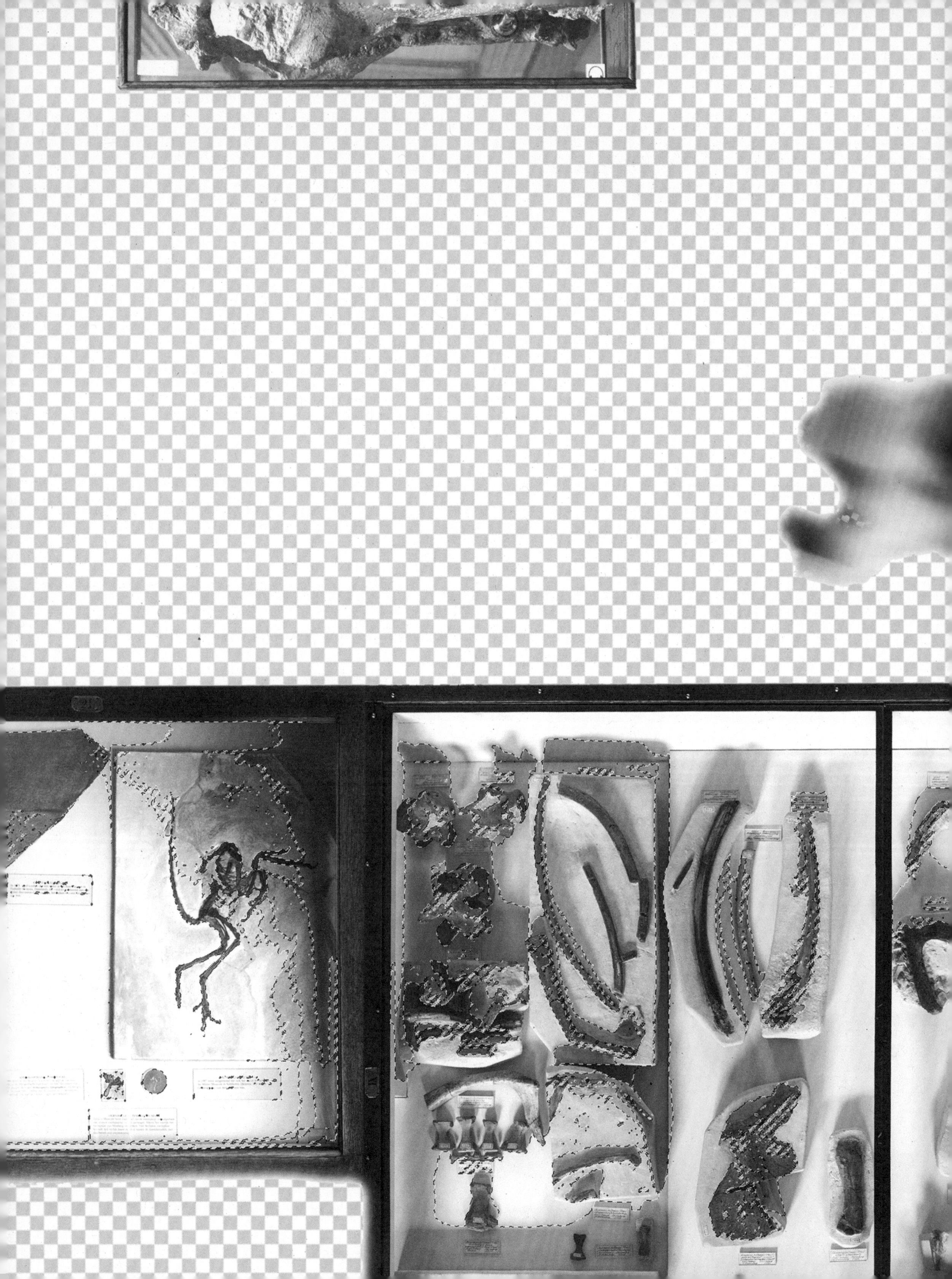

3.   Let's start at the beginning, the cornerstone of Korfmann's language: the top-down perspective of the photographic images. The photos were taken straight from above the shop floor. Hidden from the spectator's eye, dozens of photographs of the floor are then merged into one image in a complex work of composition.

The top-down perspective is easier to experience than to analyse though. What actually is top-down? What does it do?

'Bird's eye view' is the term most often used in the analysis of Korfmann's work. Or a drone view, a helicopter view. But you might just as well call it the view of the omniscient narrator, the scientific view or God's view.

The bird's eye view stresses the freedom of vision in respect to what is being seen. The bird liberates itself from all the swarming down below. Unless it is a raptor with eyes prying for fair game that soon, in one swoop, will become captured prey. Eventually, neither option seems to apply to the central perspective of Back Stages, which emphatically engages with the shop floor it portrays and certainly has no detached or murderous relation to it.

The metaphor of the drone or the helicopter brings along a connotation of power and control. It can't be a coincidence that the photographs on which the compositions have been based were not made with a drone but with the camera mounted on a long old-fashioned pole. Old-fashioned craftmanship is inherent to the project. For certain, Back Stages doesn't speak of ascendancy. Even when you listen very closely, you won't hear the annoying thump of the drone motor anywhere in the picture. The artists' view is one that lives in silence and meditation. This view doesn't exert control, it enjoys its vacancy instead.

There is no omniscient narrator either: this view knows little and wonders about many things. It lets the story tell itself rather than to direct it from the outside. Nor is it a scientific view. It doesn't want to seek or find an objective, underlying truth. God's view? No way. In the end, God will always be a judging machine.

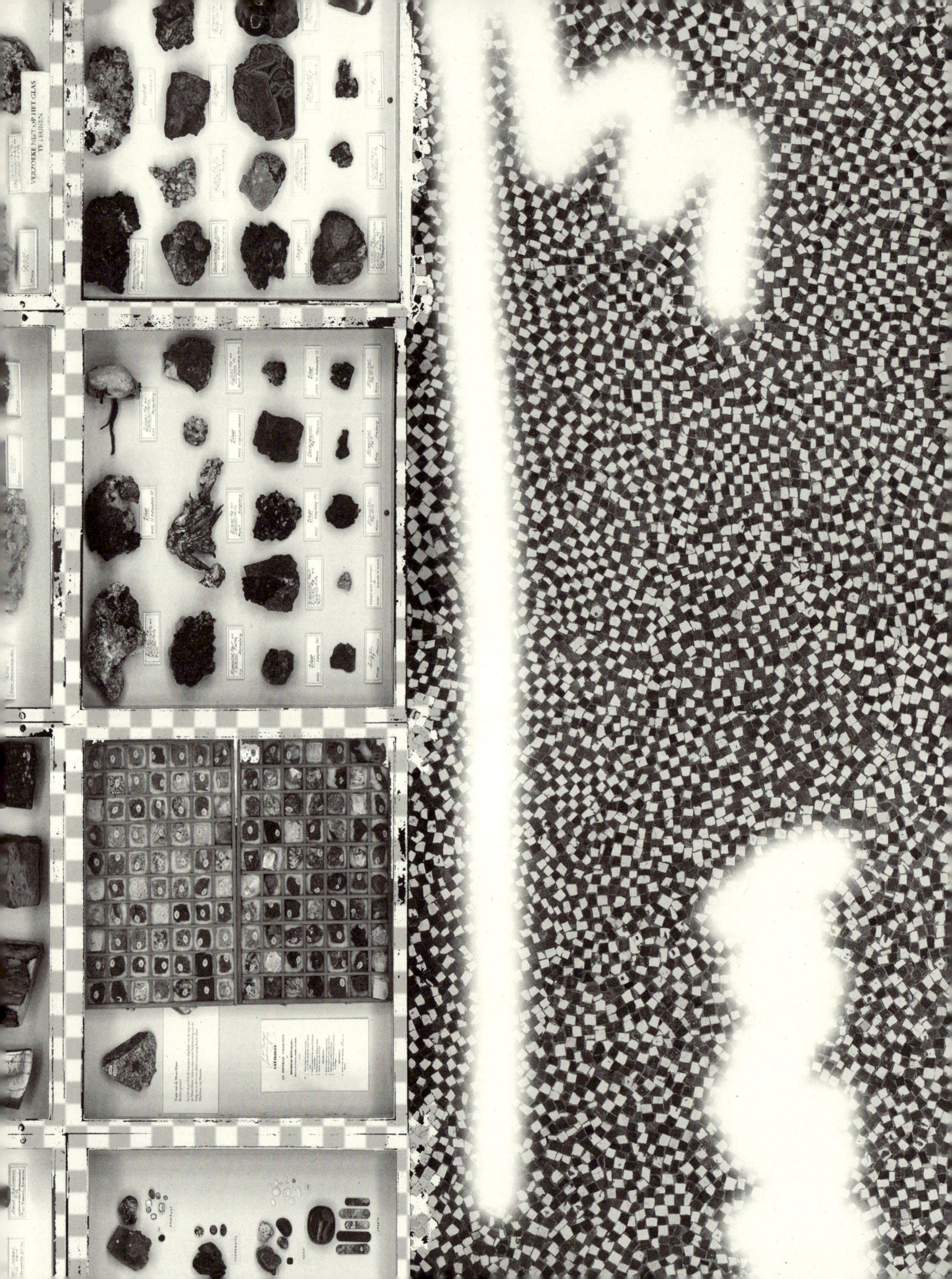

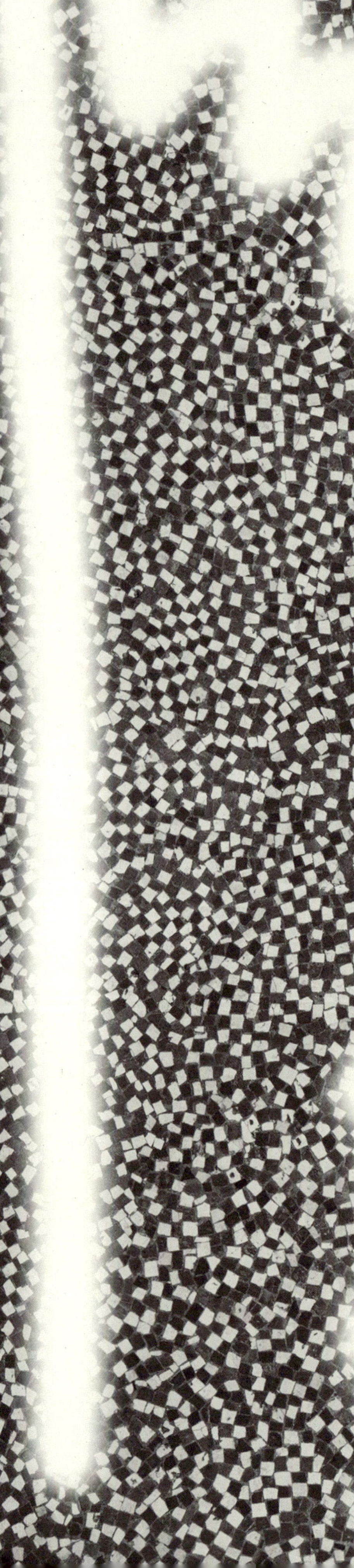
VERZOEKE NIET OP HET GLAS TE LEUNEN

Who may or may not enter the heavens? Here, propositions about good and evil are entirely absent. There is no judgement, and certainly no sentence.

But what kind of view is it then? It is a patient, compassionate human view. Not focused on plunder, control, power or judgment but on mutual encounter.

It is a view that – and I'm taking a rather intuitive and speculative leap here – is being directed from below. It's the floor that invites the artists to approach and then to take some distance again. It is a view that zooms in and out.
The view seems to be part of a body carried by the up-draught, rising warm air pockets. A free gliding, airborne view. A view hovering above the shop floor.

I could take a more technical approach to the problematic miracle of the view. If I correctly observe my own visual experience of the works in Back Stages, I can discern four different visual movements from the perspective of the audience.
There is the top-down line of sight, following the selection of the directors. From that side the photo-painting looks three-dimensional. There is a clear distance to the shop floor scenery and the labourers. The spectator's view is zooming in and out along this vertical axis.
In the gallery, however, the audience also looks at the artwork at eye level. Here, the view is confronted with a two-dimensional canvas, an abstract colour painting. This, in turn, can be scanned up-close or observed in its entirety. It's a surface investigation of a flat world.
I think that a combination of these directions of view forms the basis for the visual experience of the audience.

The artists select a landscape to explore. The scene of artisanal labour. They construct an artistic position of a free-floating body that communicates with the scenery. The viewer then actively engages with the resulting images.

The interplay of the artist and the audience brings about a playfulness that lays the foundation for the mellow, pleasant feeling evoked by looking at this work. It has something childlike and game-like to it. 'Now you see Freud's head, now you perceive the brow and the nose as a naked woman.' 'By the way, where is Wally? Well, hidden somewhere in this jumble of figures and colours.' Now you see a colour painting. But now, suddenly, you see a supporter of a football team. Und kein Ende. Viewing and gaming pleasure assured.

Korfmann and Pfeifer's imagination is like a dance. A nimble choreography is operating in the compositions. With an up-tempo beat (and – forgive me the expression – a lot of synths) in a site-specific environment: that of the artisanal shop floor.

That concludes the most important arsenal of directing in this project. A freely hovering point of view, a strategy to actively involve the audience, a nimble, up-tempo, dancing composition technique.

Is the initial journey, from labour to desirable labour to the craft-manship of art, invalidated or made redundant by this train of thought?
I don't think so.

By composing images based on documentary material, the Back Stages project shows a close affinity between the production of art and early industrial manufacturing processes. To the extent that labour is collective, intense, intimate and knowledge-sharing, it can be good labour. Labour conditions, that is, where the free imagination of the artist can get to work and invite the viewer to actively participate in the creation of meaning.

To what end do Korfmann and Pfeifer deploy their arsenal?
Why did they conceive and elaborate this project?

Ultimately, Back Stages is a self-questioning of the artists. What is our work? What is our place in society? Unsurprisingly, Korfmann and Pfeifer arrive at the implicit assumption that artistic practice has the potential to become a model for good labour. Labour that, at the very least, can annotate the degradation of the labour culture in our societies. With thoughtful lightness, Korfmann and Pfeifer produce beautiful photo-paintings of labour in our days.

          PAUL DE BRUYNE

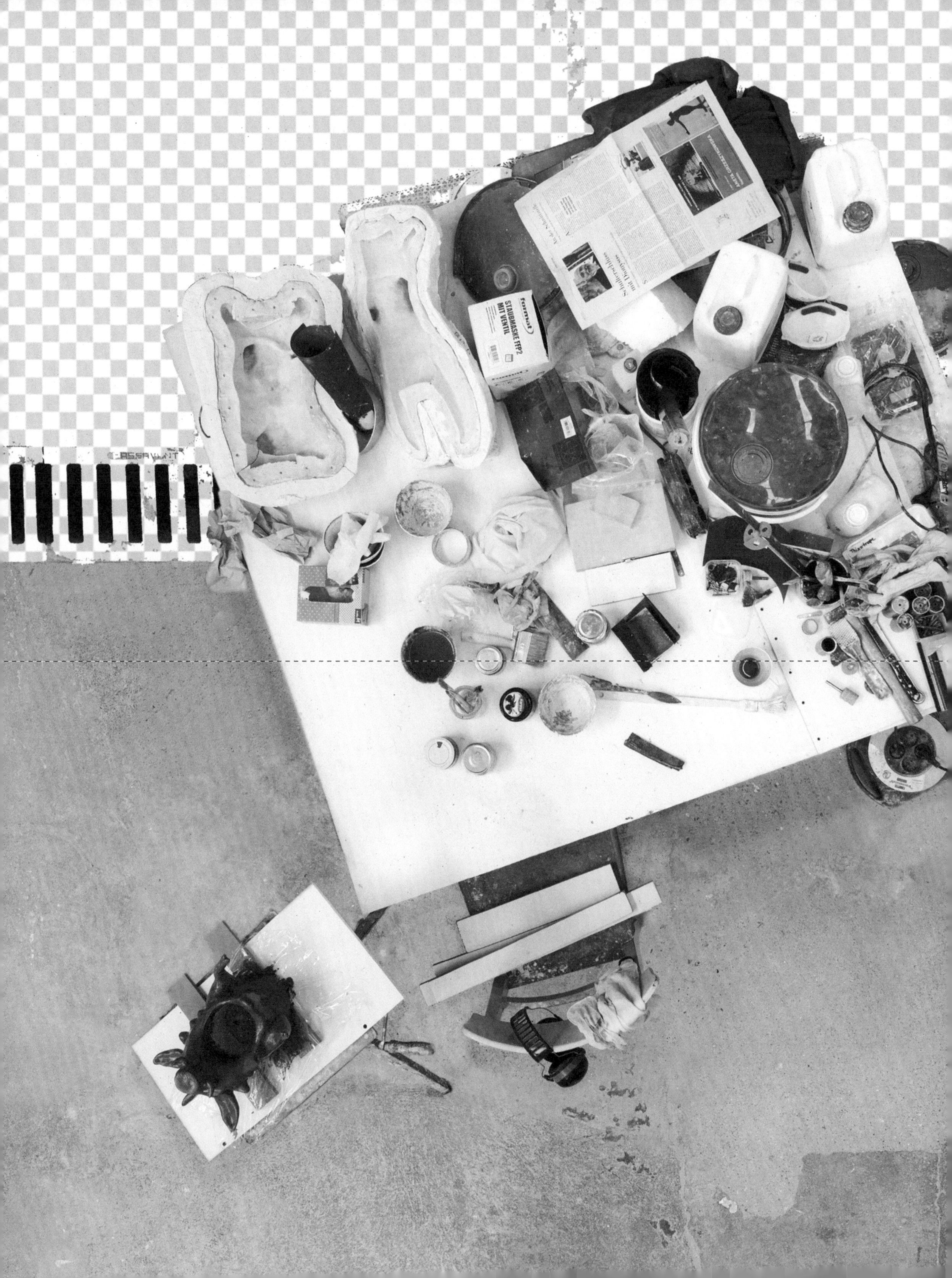

STAUBMASKE FFP2
MIT VENTIL

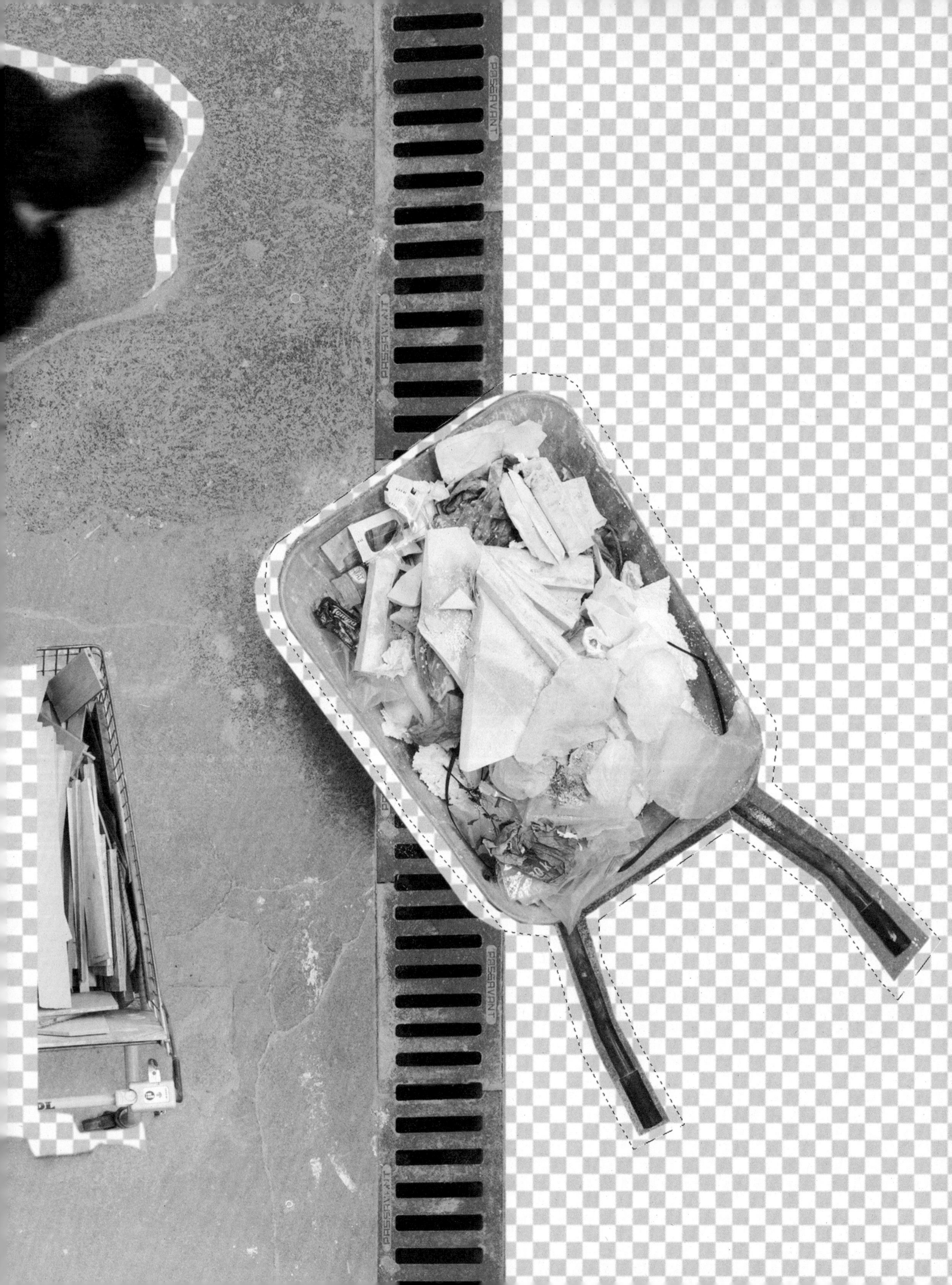

BILDHAUERWERKSTATT, BERLIN
Collaborative artists' studio space in Germany
145 × 100 cm | 57" × 39"

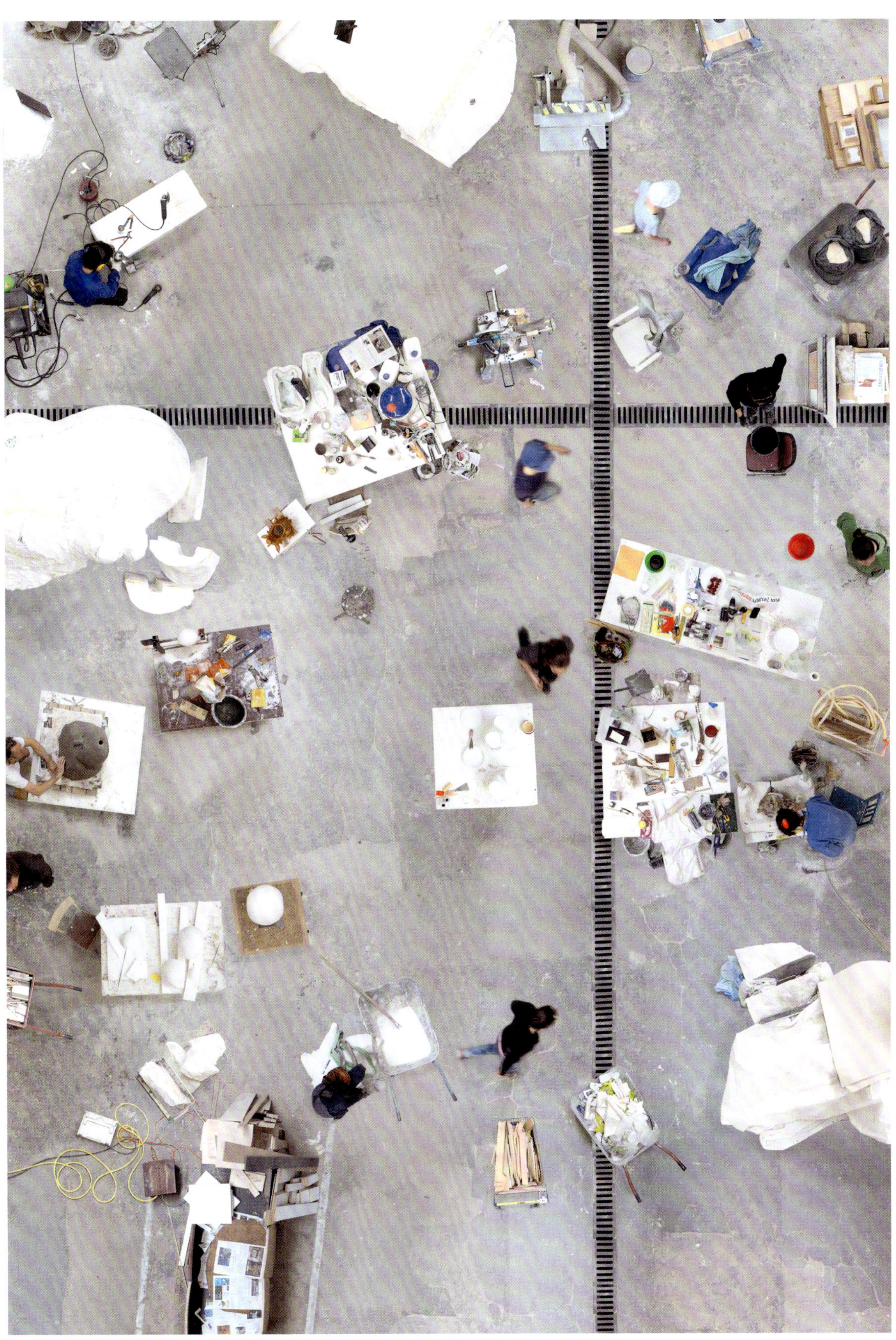

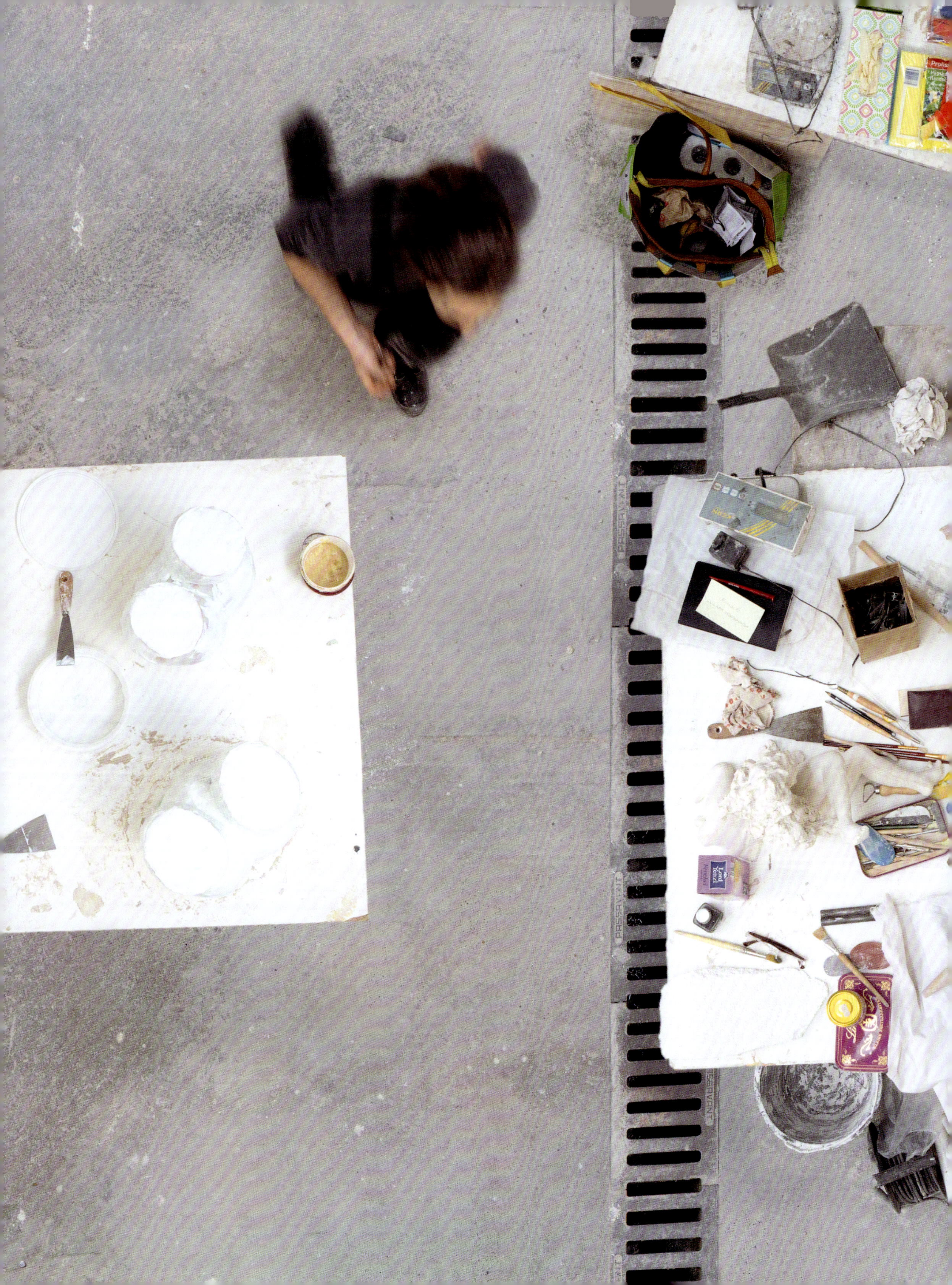

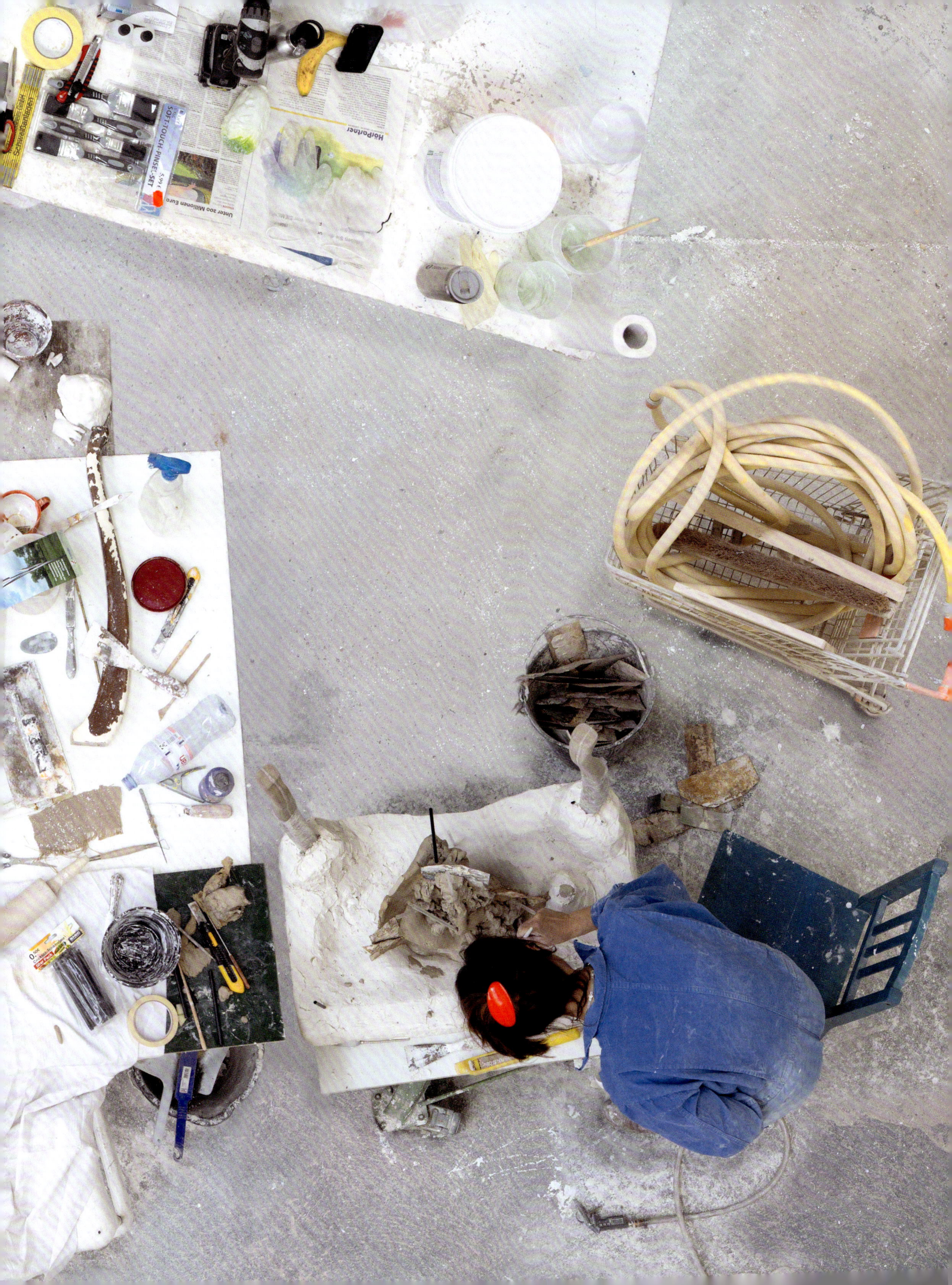

PASSAVENT

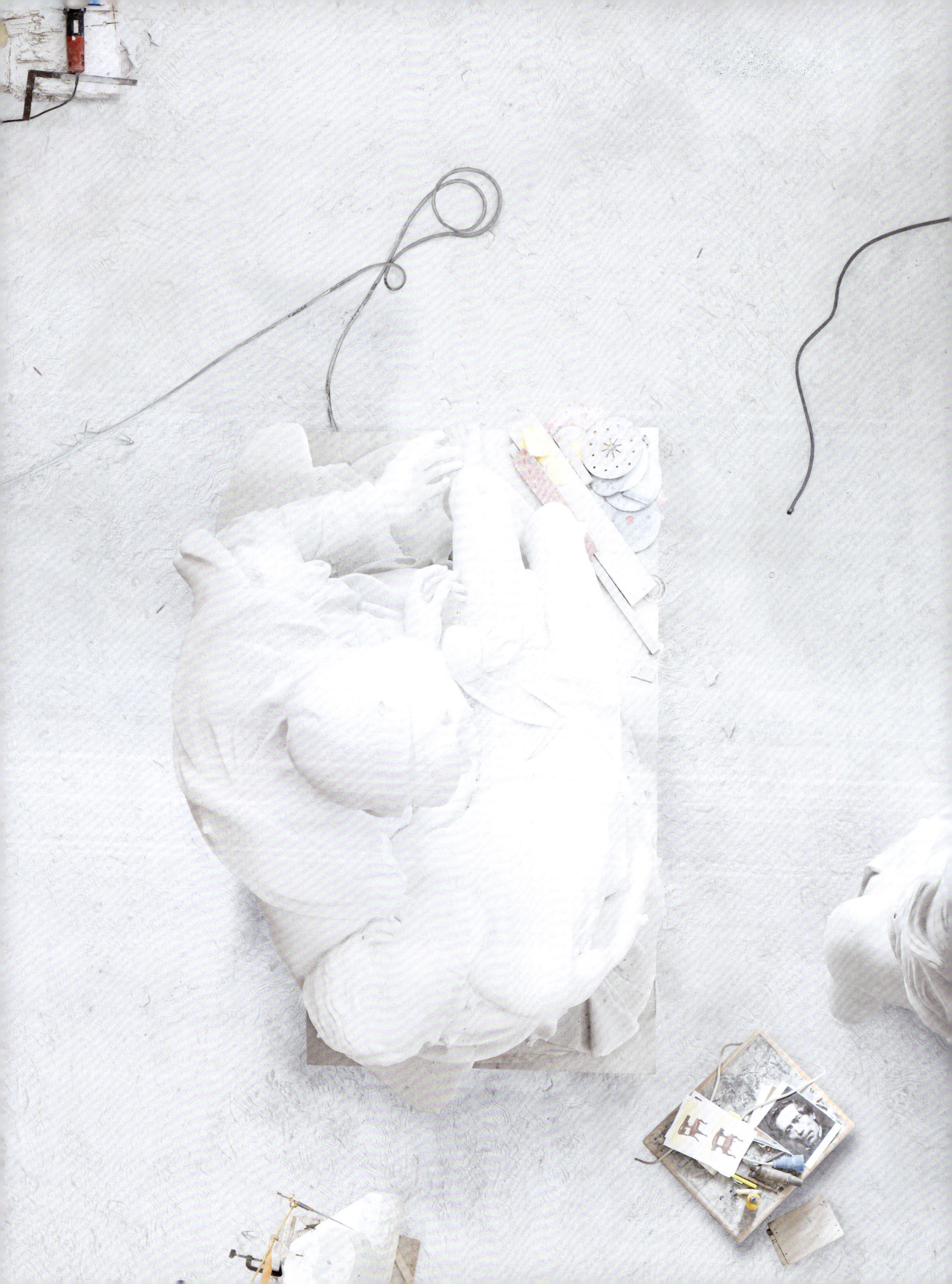

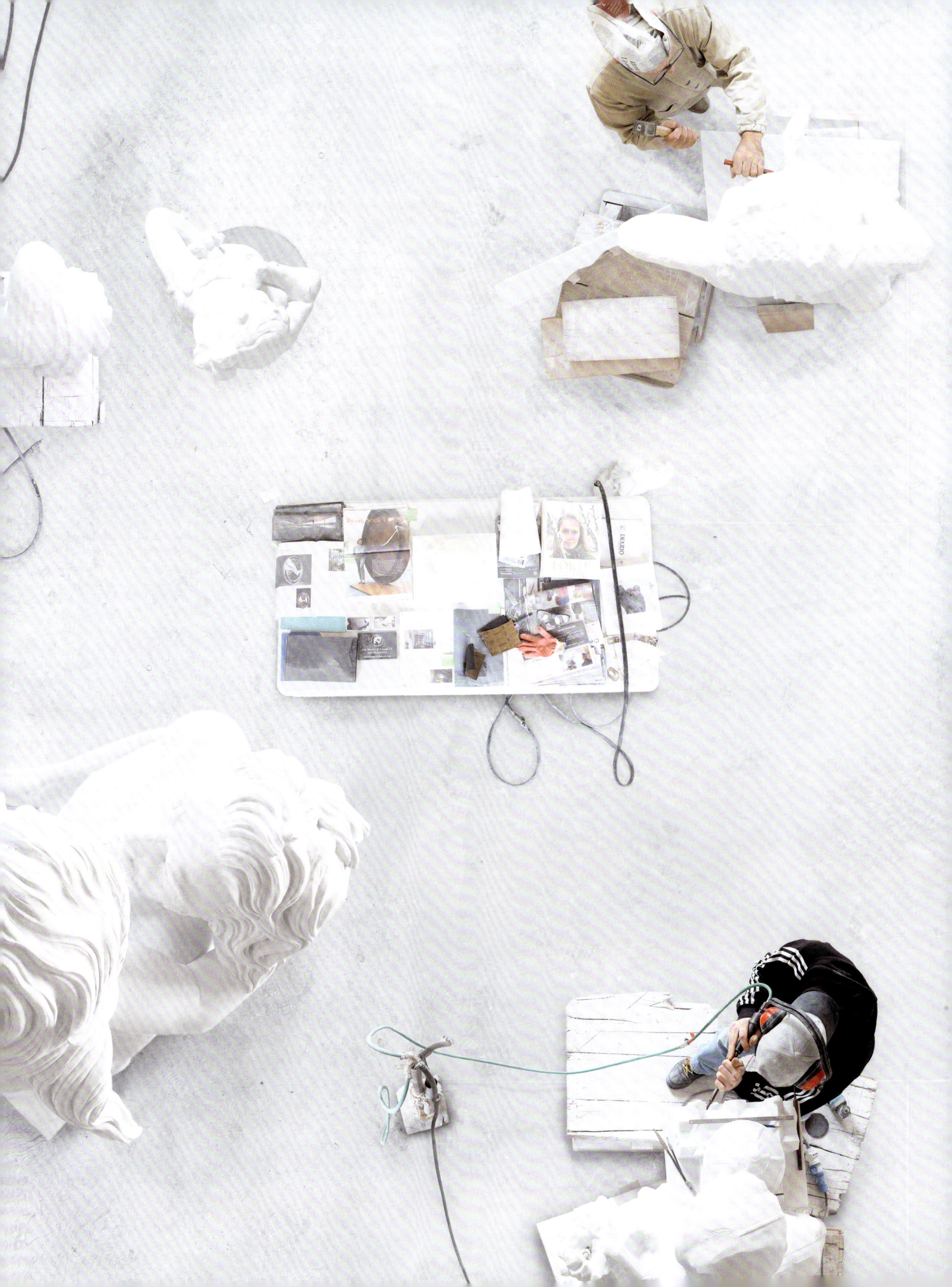

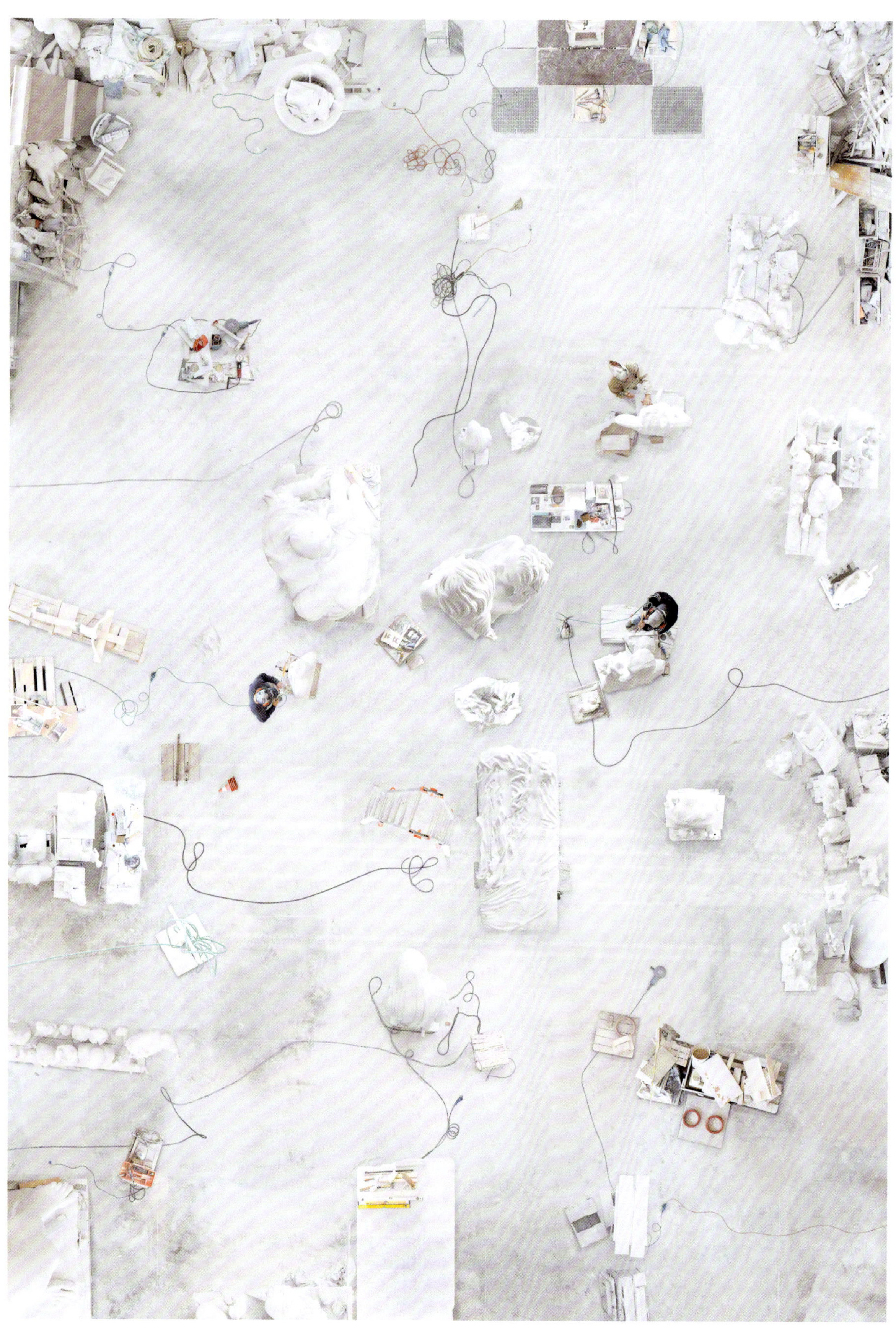

BALLET REHEARSAL, AMSTERDAM
Rehearsal of the Dutch National Ballet, the Netherlands
145 × 100 cm | 57" × 39"

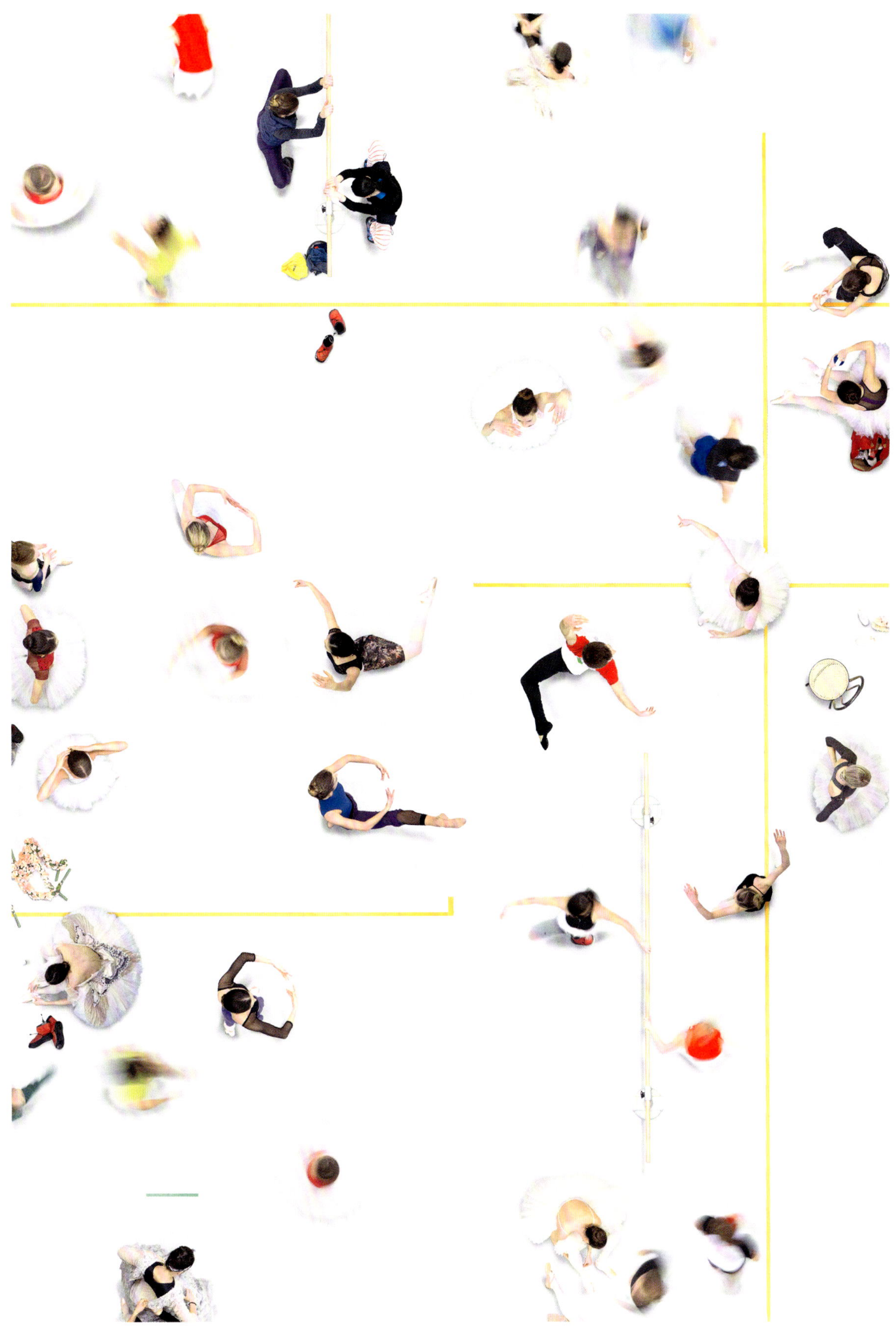

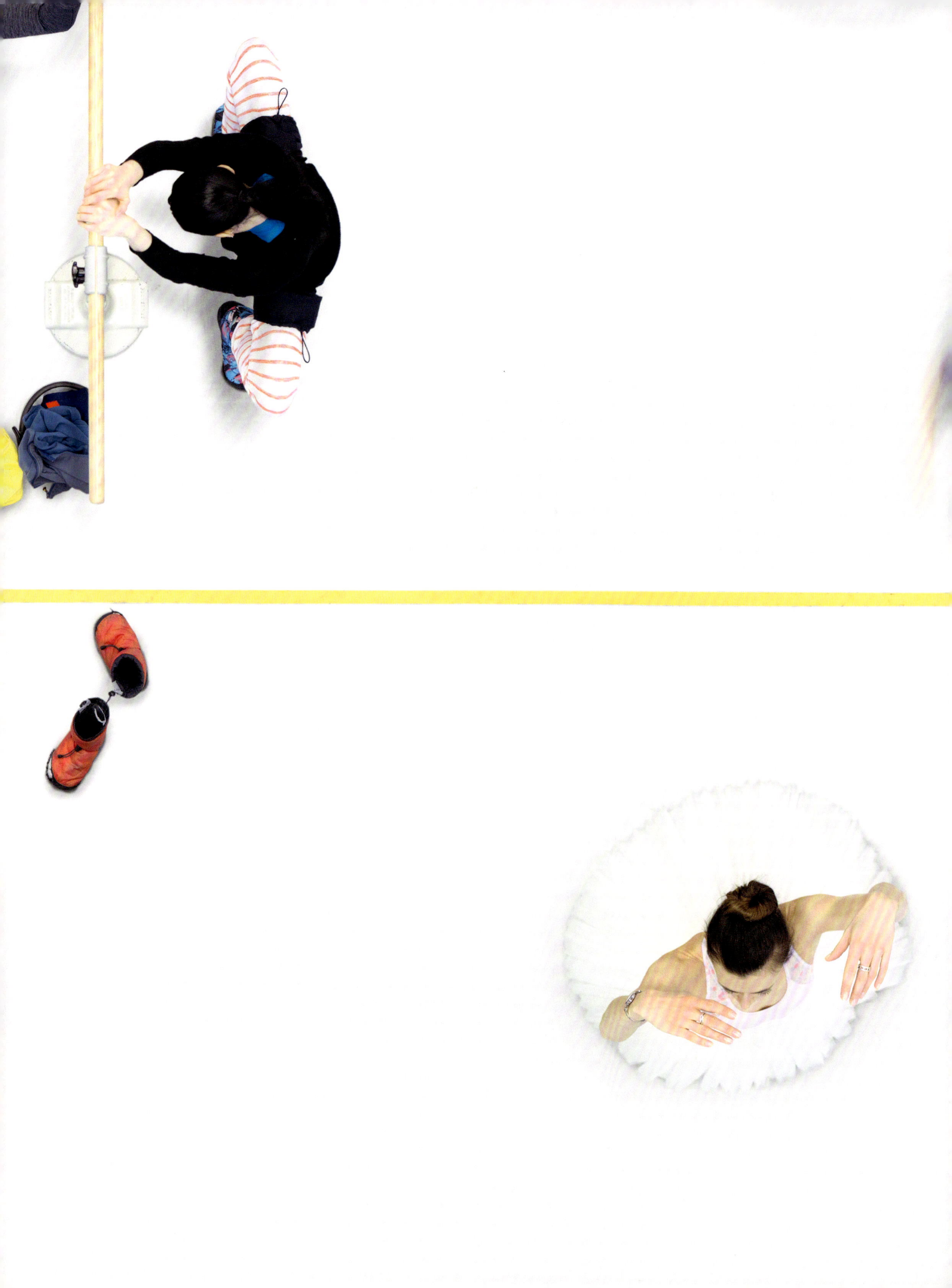

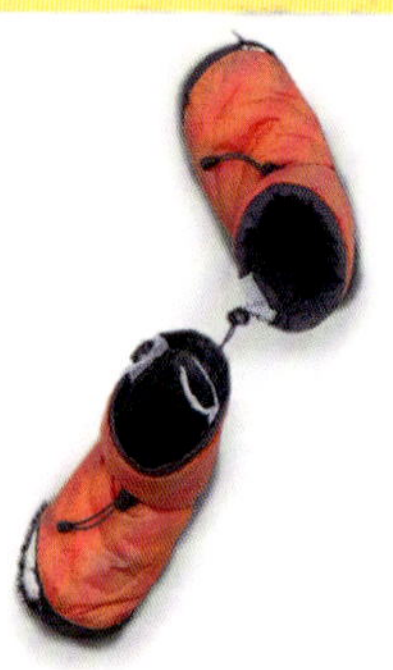
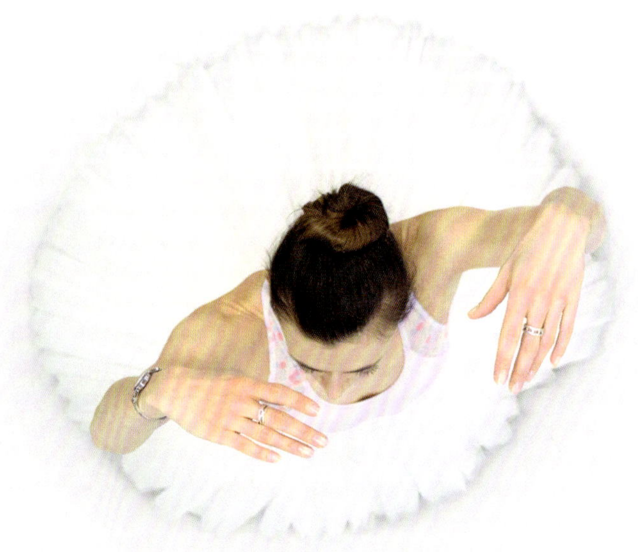

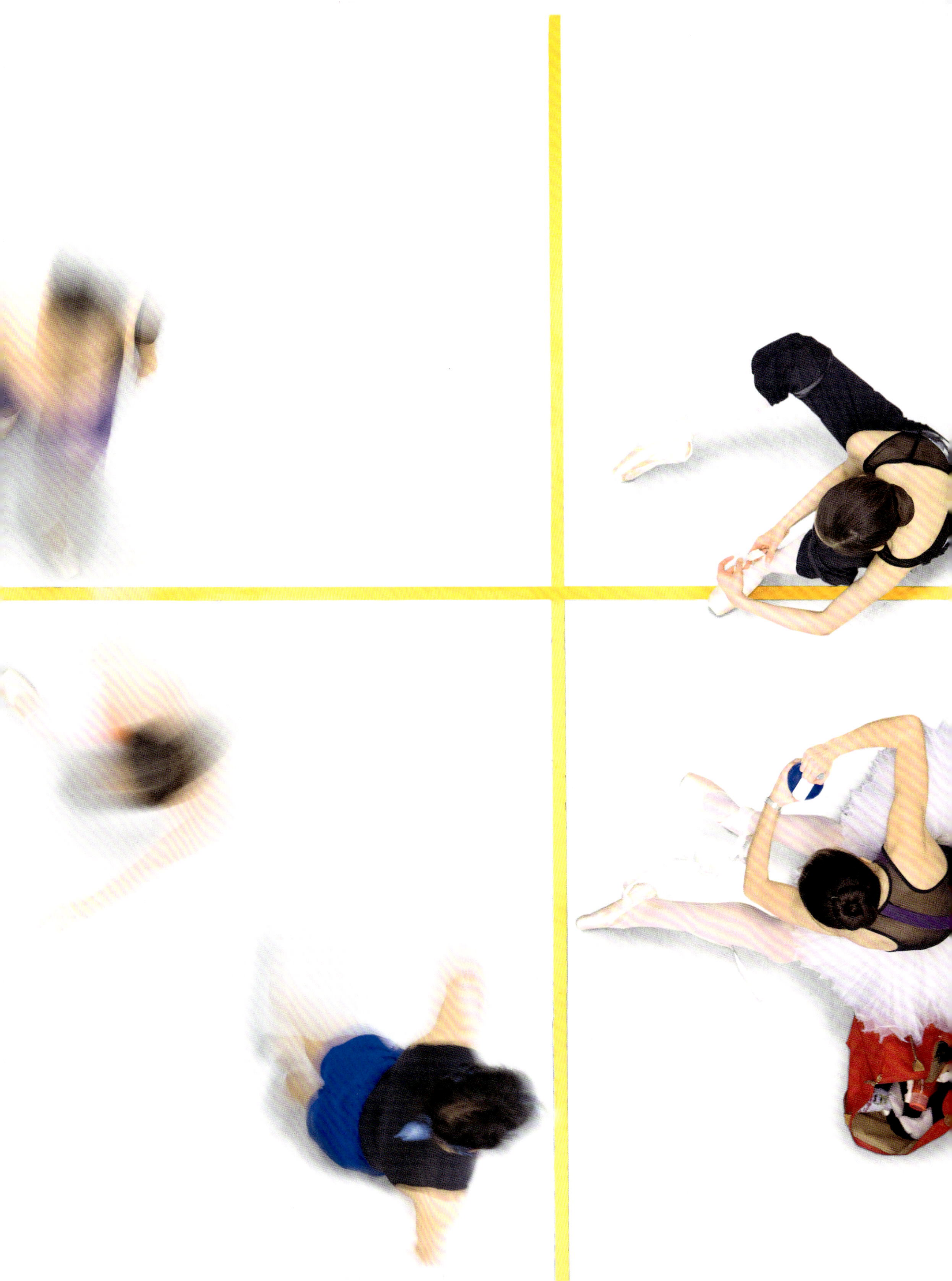

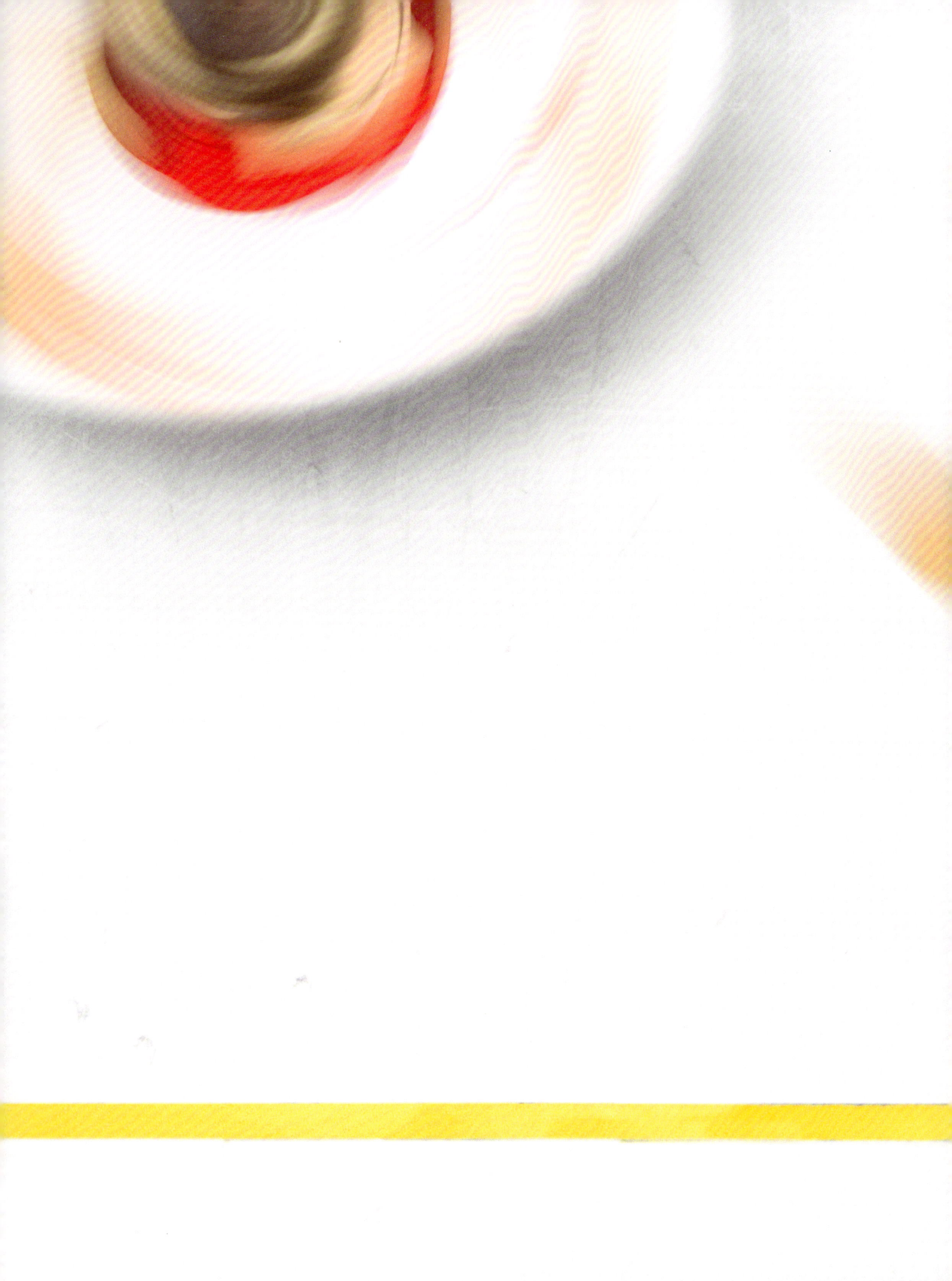

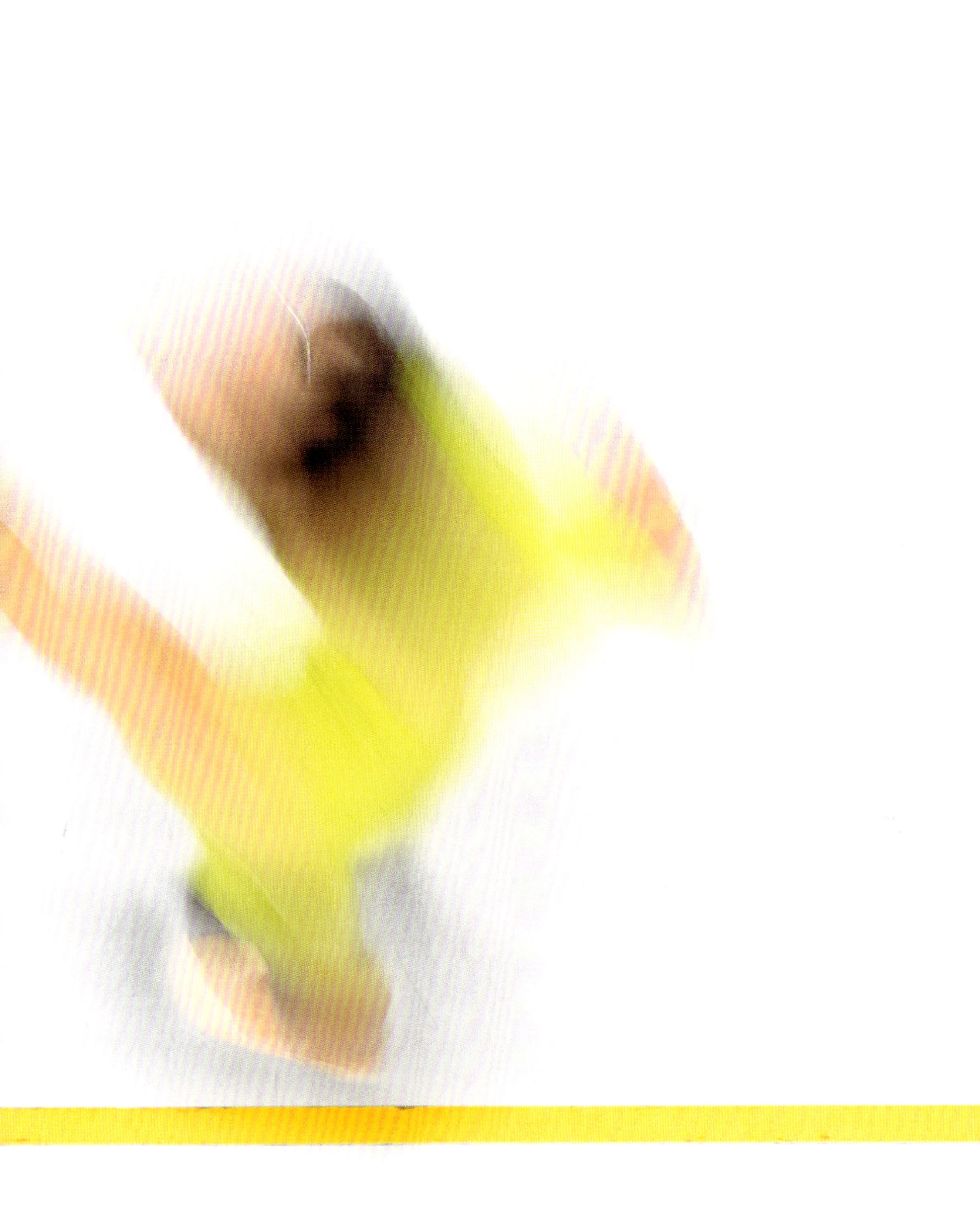

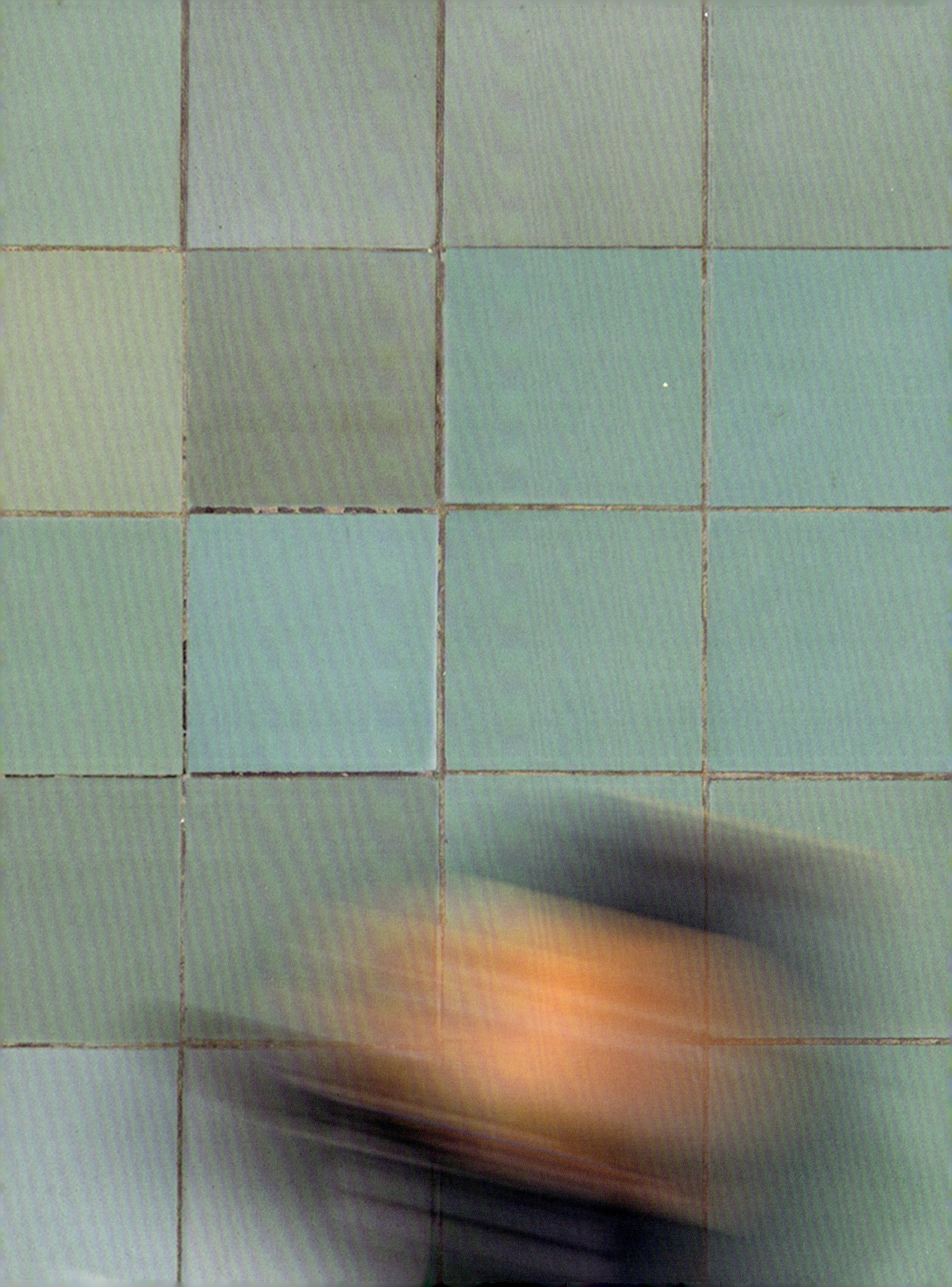

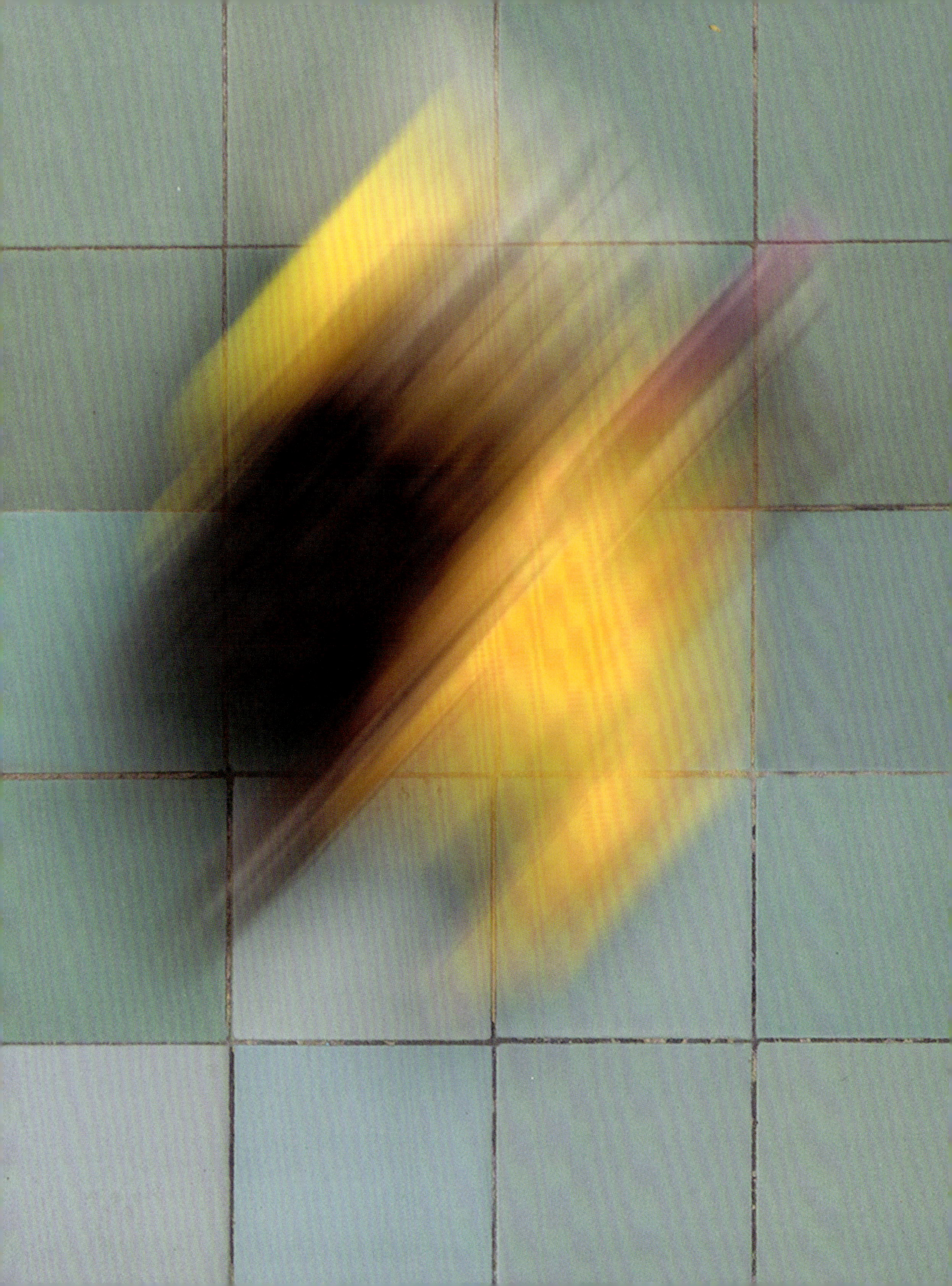

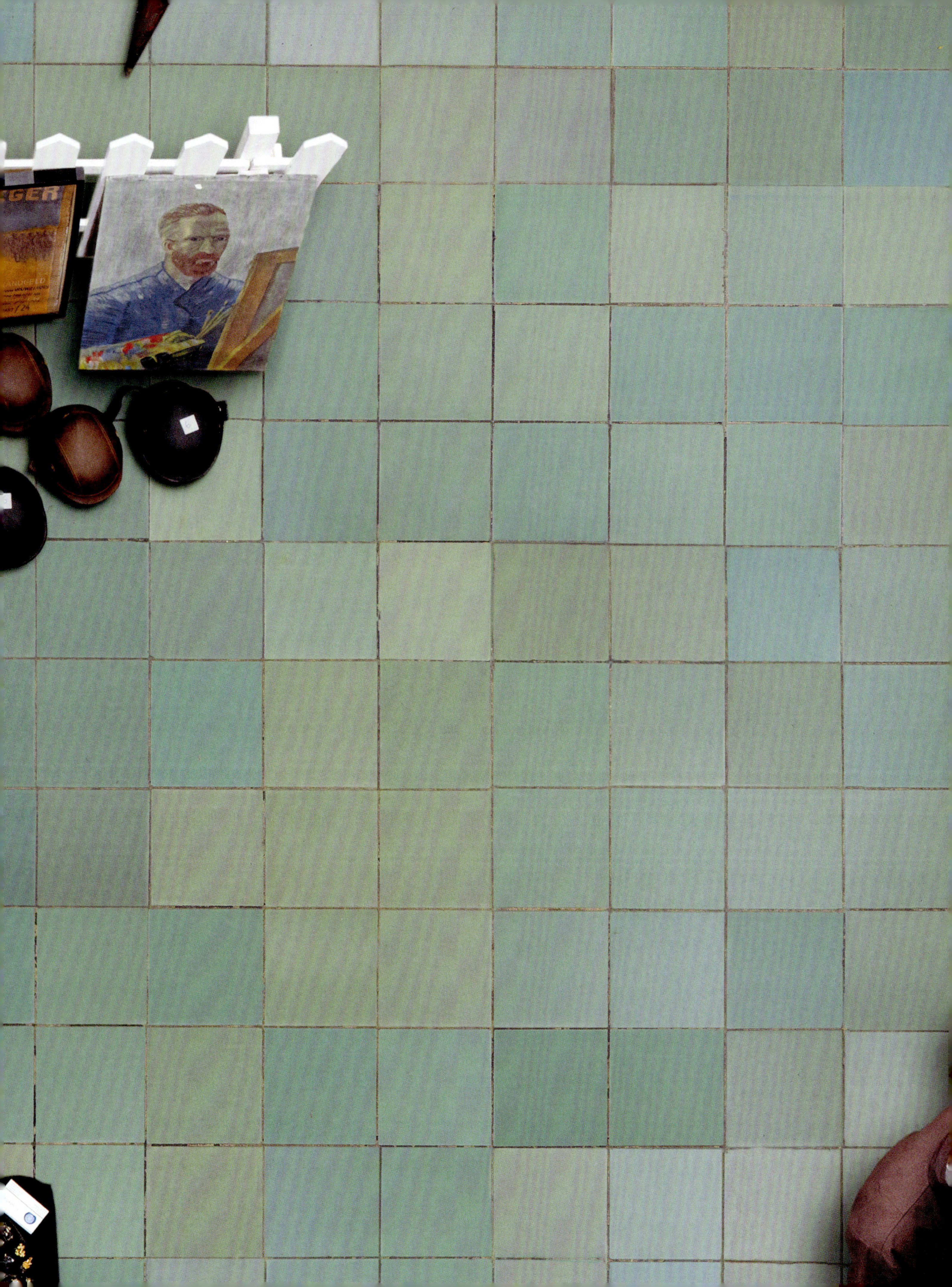

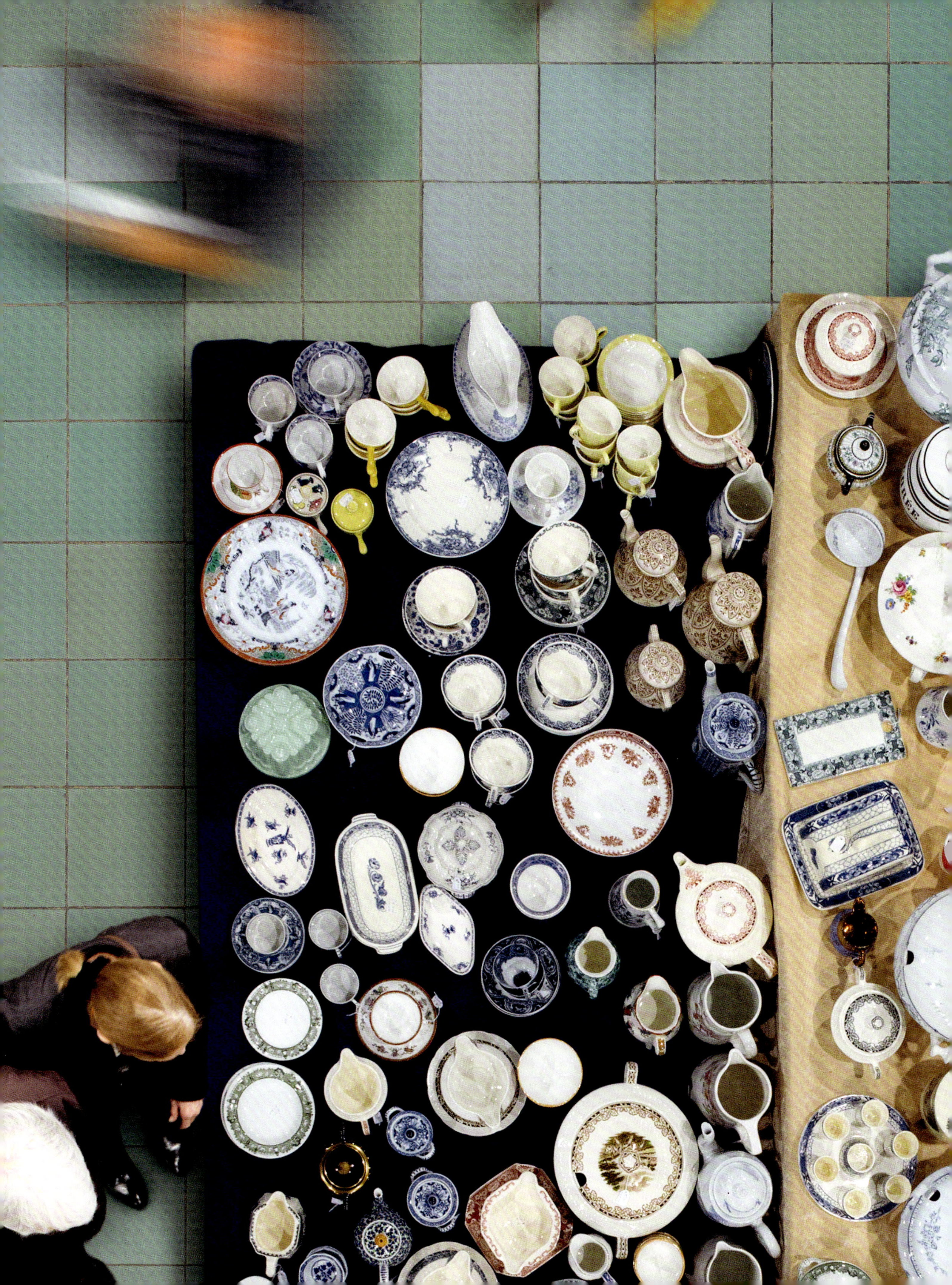

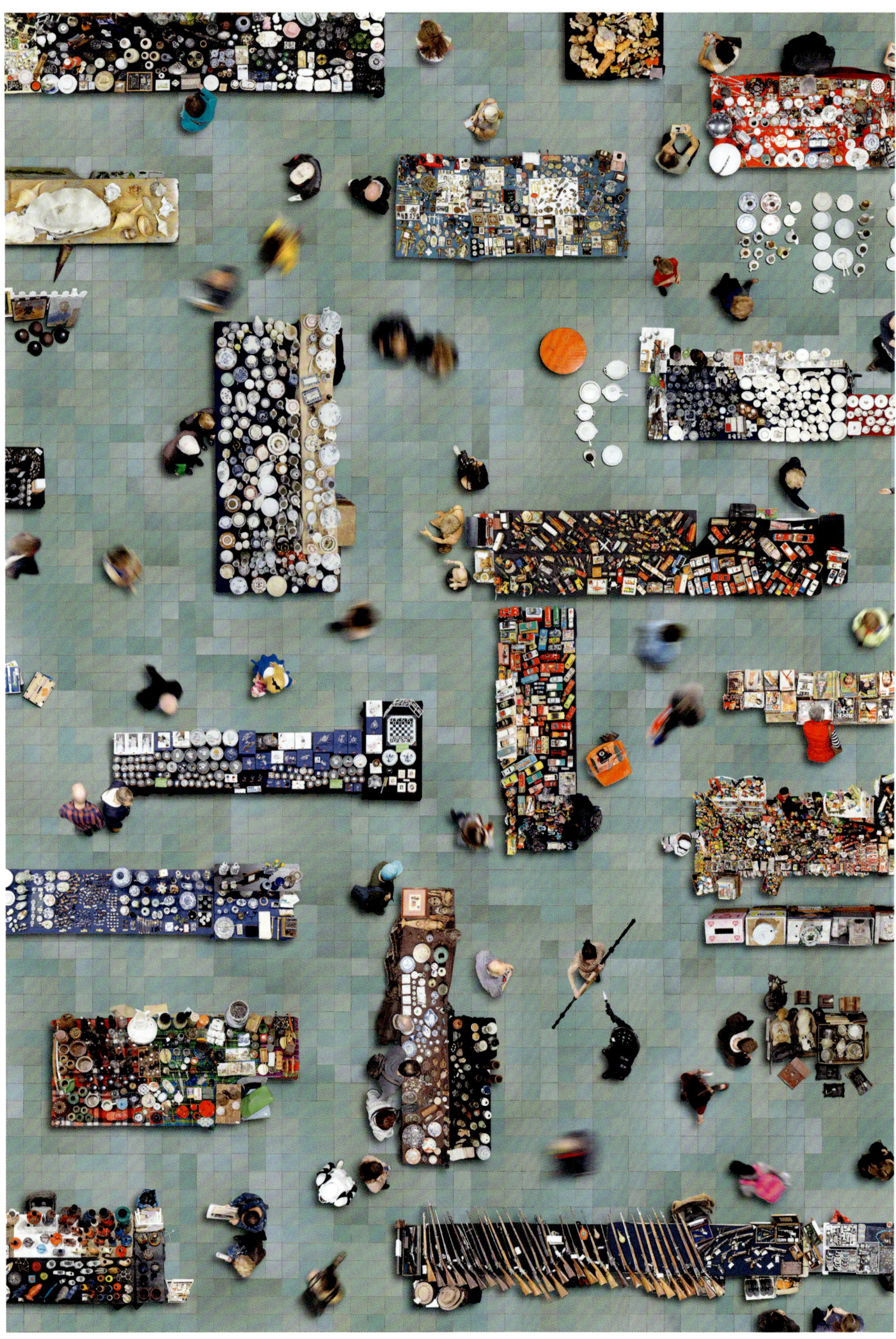

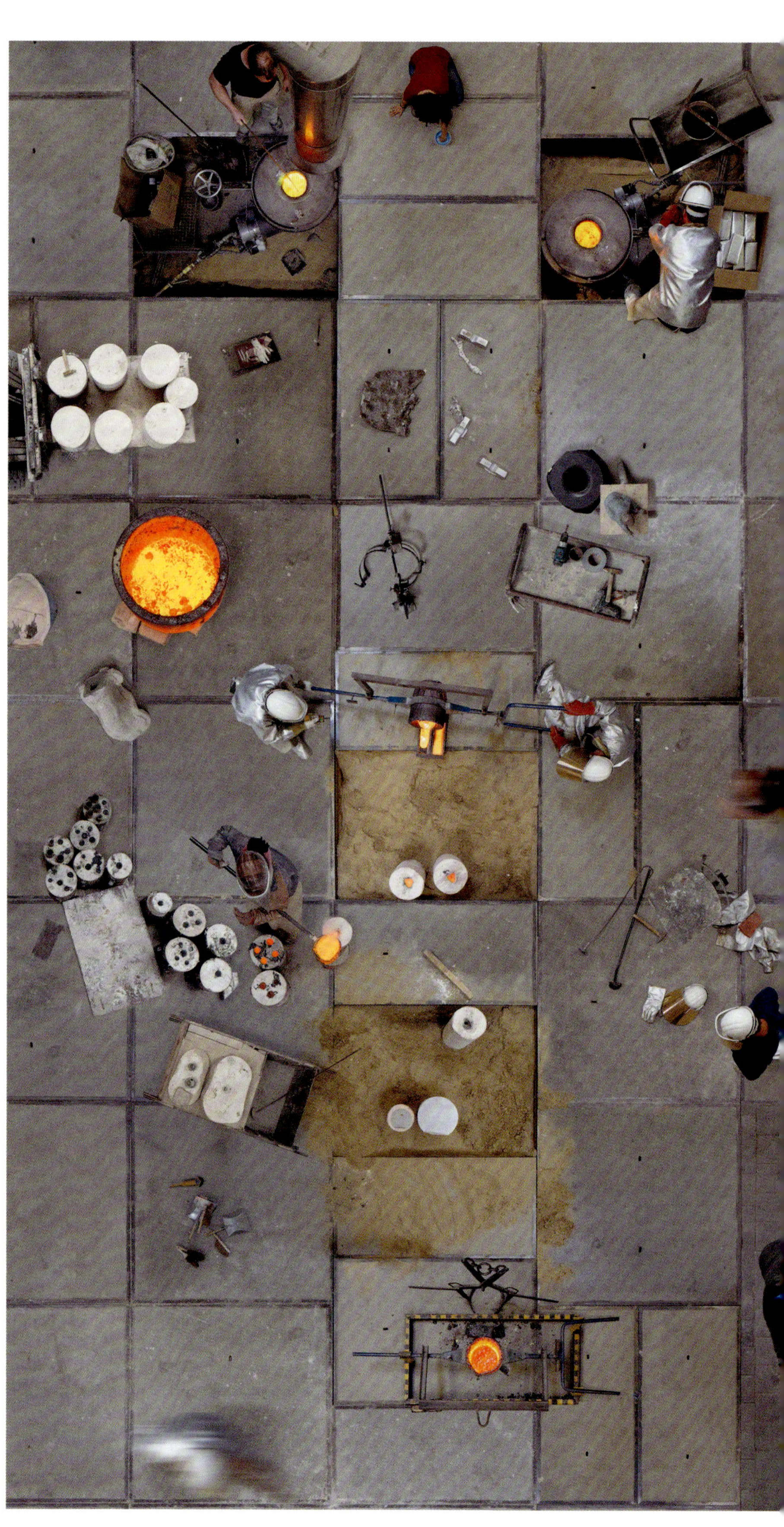

NIJHOF BEELDENSTORM, BRABANT
Bronze art foundry in the Netherlands
120 × 173 cm | 47" × 68"

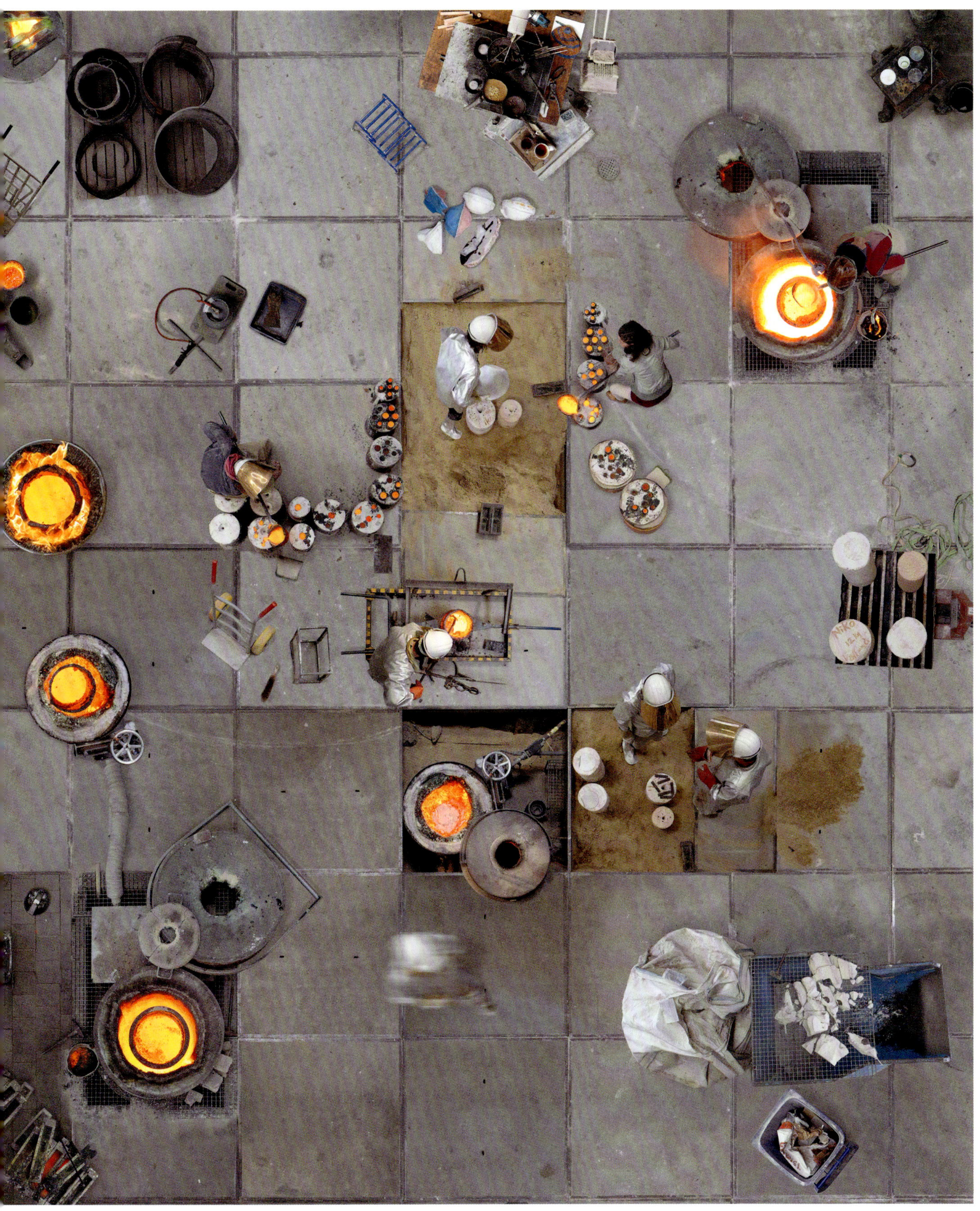

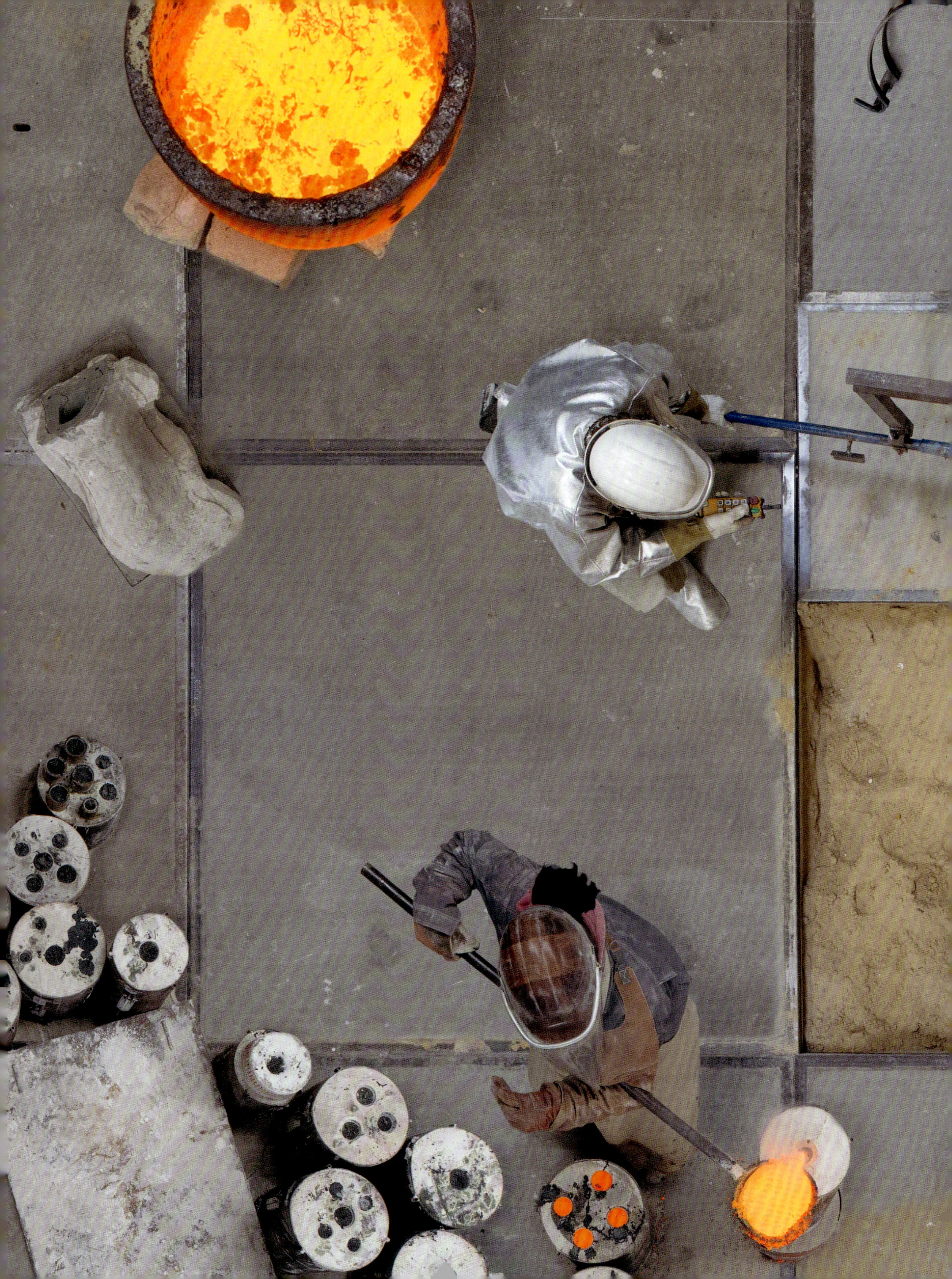

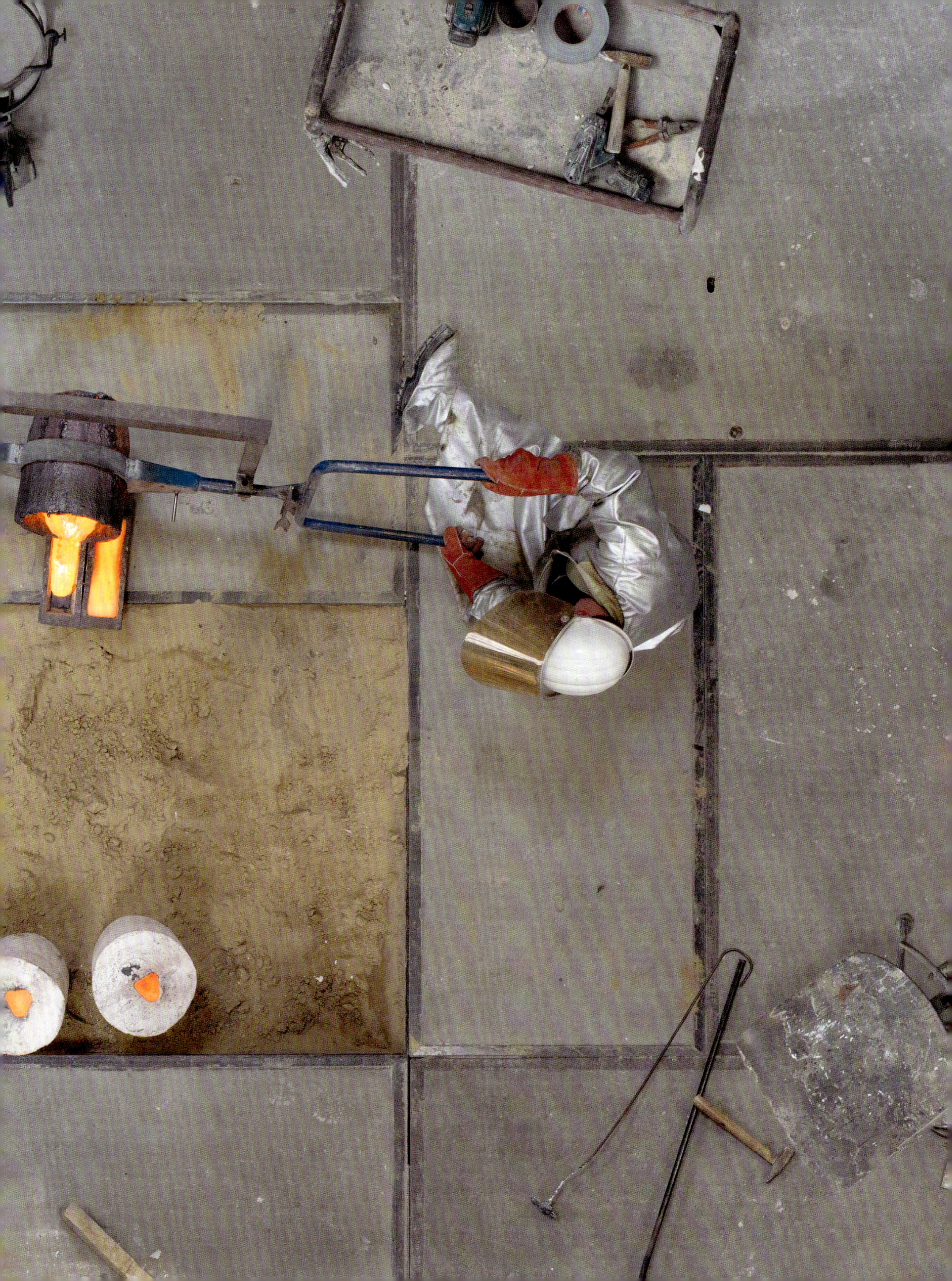

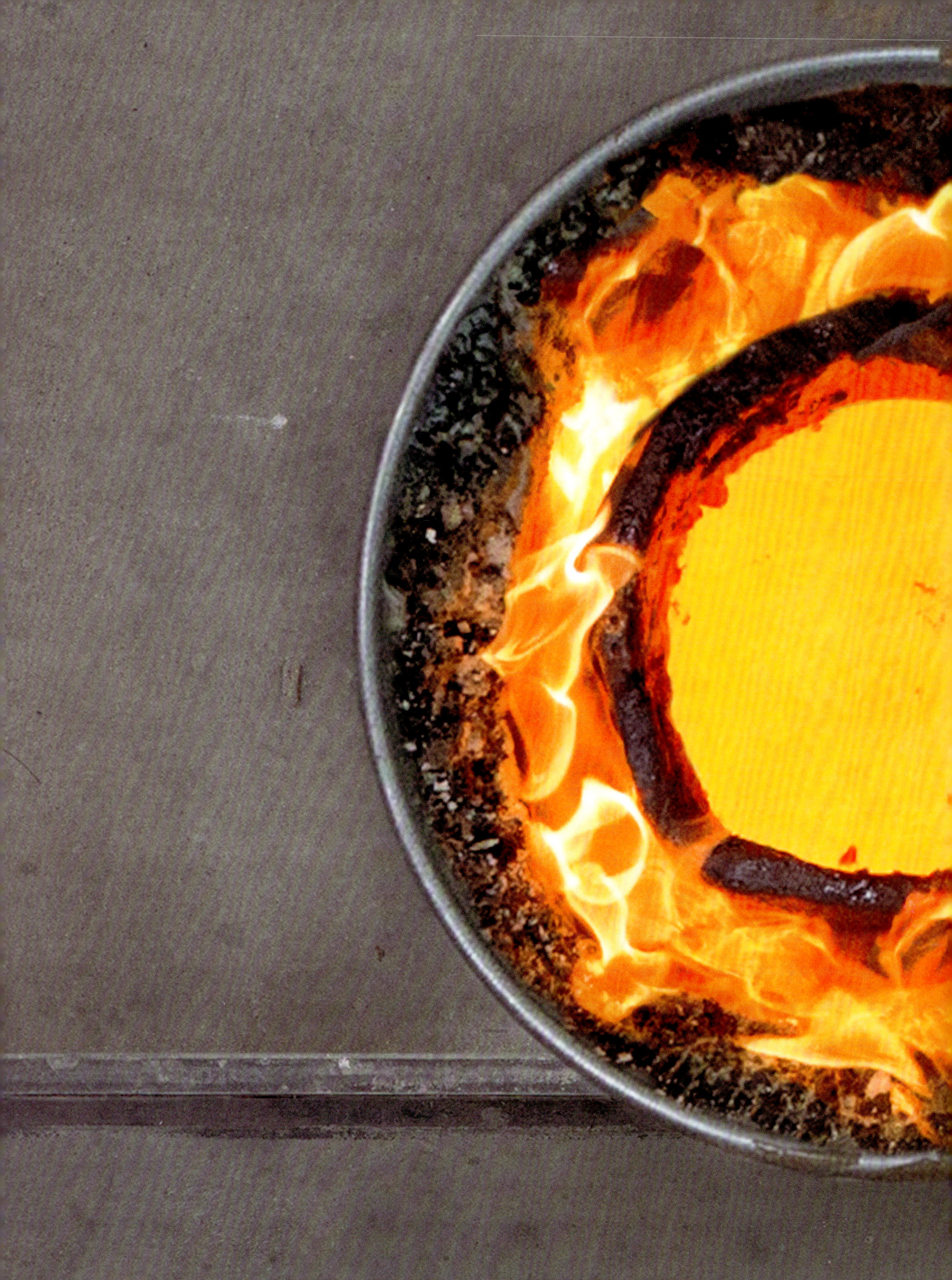

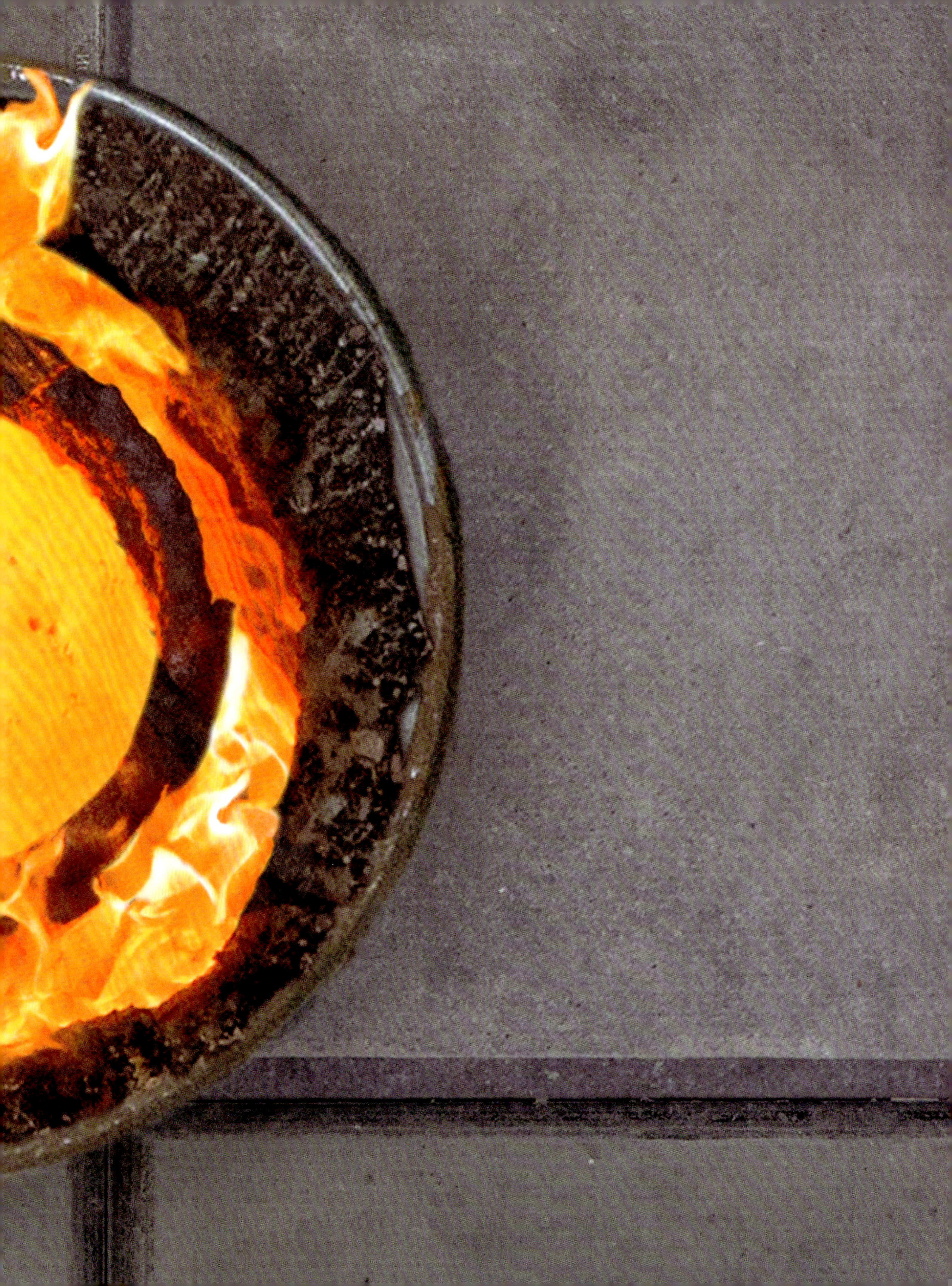

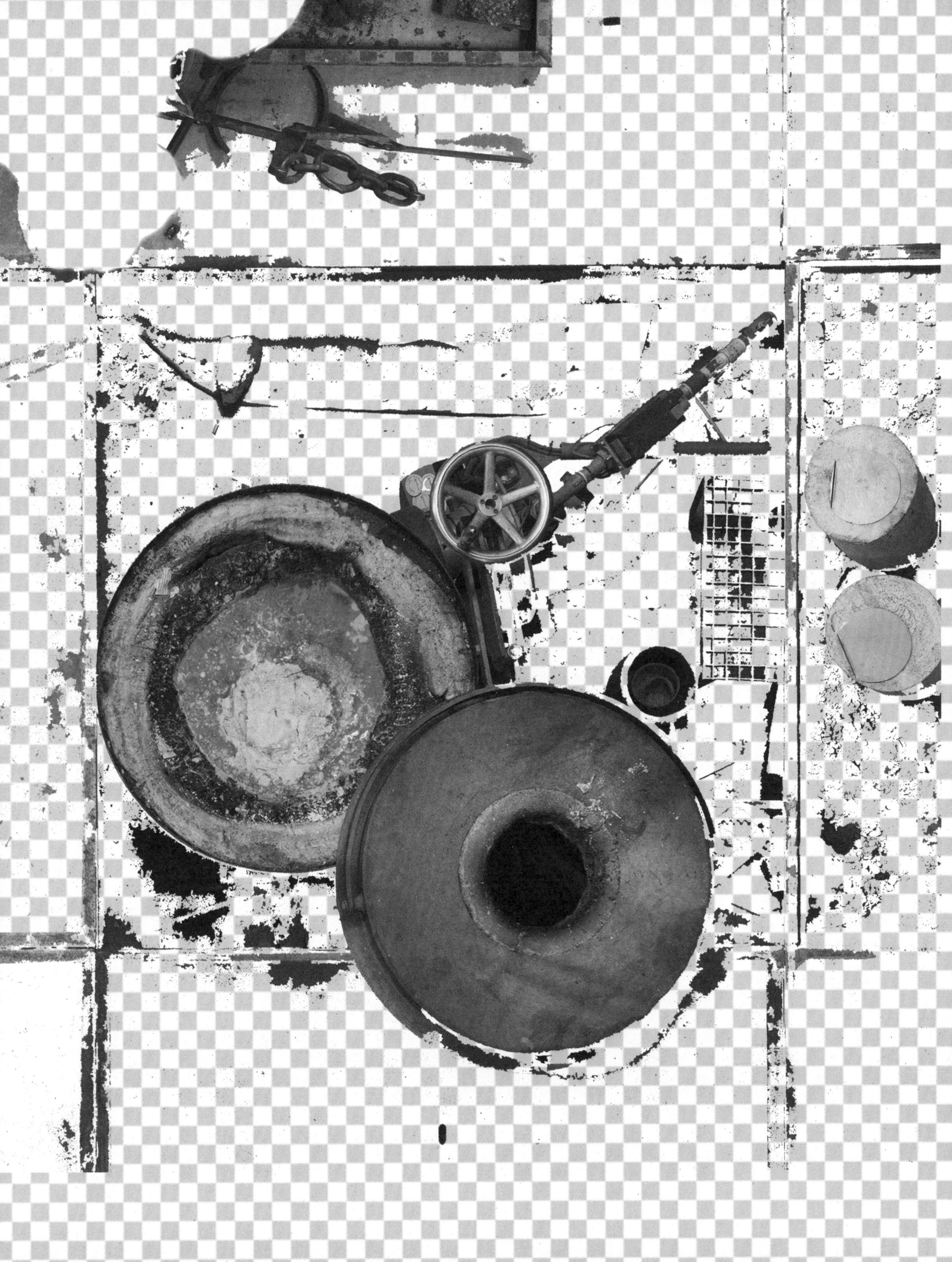

4.   Short epilogue. Two photo-compositions from the *Back Stages* series – science museum Teylers and the collectors fair – distance themselves from the production floor, towards the hall where consumers, more numerous and mobile than the labourers on the shop floor, are in command.

It is a movement away form the back stage, the studio and the rehearsal room, to the front stage. The front stage is the world of educational and financial values. The world that back stages and production places can't escape from, except in the procedure of creating them. Showing the front stages makes it abundantly clear that the *Back Stages* project has the ambience of the work in a rehearsal room. The doors are still closed for the other actors in the work field. Meaning is still emerging, the critics are far away, the labourers are not artists yet. The work remains autonomous. Just for a little while. And then real life comes peeping round the corner.

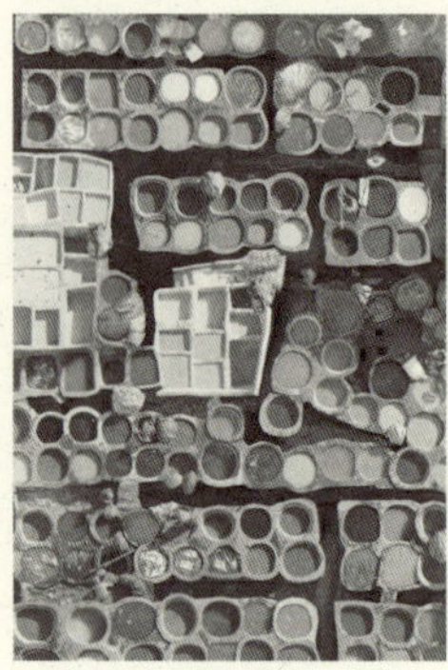

15 CHOUARA, FEZ
11th-century tannery in Morocco
173 × 120 cm | 68" × 47"

Family run cooperatives have been tanning leather in Chouara for the best part of 1000 years. Located in the old town of Fez and still fully functioning, this ancient industry has become a popular tourist destination. The basins depicted are filled with the dyes used by the workers and although the site and its surroundings are beautiful, the smells coming from it are repugnant. The reason for the strong odour is the pigeon droppings that are being used to unhair the hides. The basins in which the skins are dyed are quite large, with some pots measuring 1.50 meters in diameter. Once a week, all the dyes in the pots are renewed and the colour combinations are constantly changing. All the colours are made with natural materials such as poppy seeds and saffron.

The tannery has been an independent self-sufficient business for hundreds of years, that also includes the many shops surrounding it.

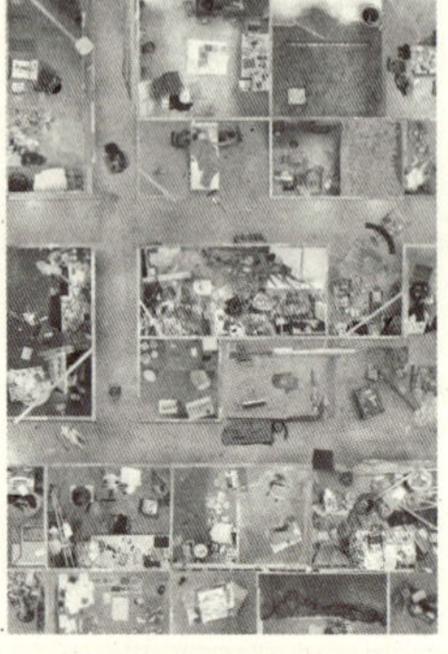

26 RIETVELD ACADEMIE, AMSTERDAM
Art academy in the Netherlands
173 × 120 cm | 68" × 47"

In this picture we see the workspaces of the Fine Art Department at the Gerrit Rietveld Academie in Amsterdam. The studios are located in a huge warehouse. Katrin and Jens were fascinated by the way the space was divided; every student has their own tiny workroom that they can use to experiment and explore.

The structure of the space reminded them of the architecture of art fairs. The design of the space, basically just a square box, seems to be a constant companion for the artwork; first in the art schools and then at the fairs where the market is taking over the creative space. Yet there is a vast contrast between the origin of the artistic endeavour and the high-end commercial venues.

Another notable aspect is the different kinds of materials the students use. In the middle of the picture we see a student at work, the floor smirched with paint, the space scattered

with cans, brushes, canvasses and even a water gun; in the top right a whole studio floor is covered with a grass lawn; in another there are keyboards and two guys are sewing a huge piece of fabric. The details reveal the bustling creativity of the students and the organised chaos that is so typical of an art school.

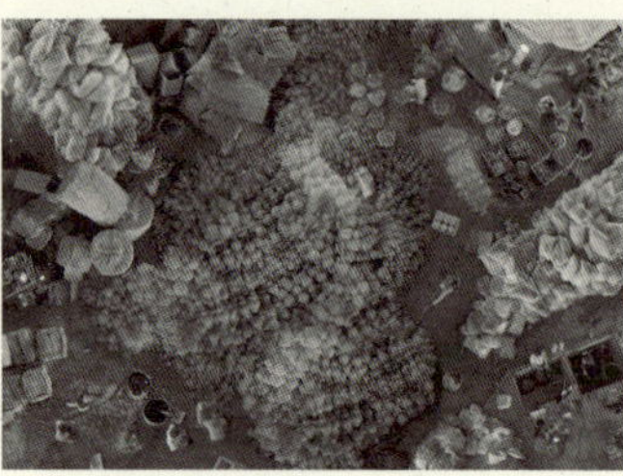

37 GLASS, ANXI
Glass factory in China
150 × 216 cm | 59" × 85"

This glass factory in Anxi, southern Fujian province, is a family business that mainly produces hand-made mould-blown glass. The facilities in the factory are very basic. It is situated on a hill outside a small village, with one large furnace and a shabby roof covering the workspace. The batch for making the glass is piled up in large bags all over the work floor. It's a pretty chaotic place; the heat from the furnace is intense, as is the sound from the fans that are used in an attempt to cool the space. Because the factory uses coal to fire the kilns, the floor is pitch black. The unhealthy environment of the factory is in stark contrast with the shiny blue, emerald and crystal-like glass it produces.

Small workshops like this come and go, bound as they are to the changes of an unpredictable economy.

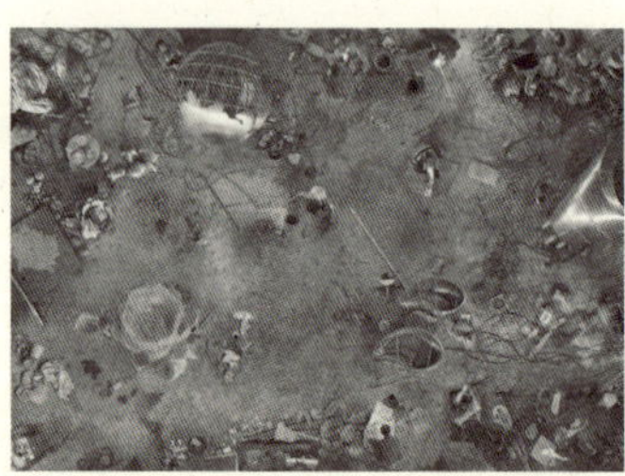

38 STAINLESS STEEL, XIAMEN
Stainless steel fabrication
workshop for sculpture in China
120 × 173 cm | 47" × 68"

The stainless steel fabrication workshop in Xiamen, China is an enormous chaos where materials slither across the ground like snakes. A huge steel globe shines as if it is already finished, while a steel lotus flower, situated to the left, is wrapped in plastic, awaiting a final touch. Jens had a small series of sculptures made in this workshop. This was one of the first pictures that Katrin and Jens created for Back Stages. Fascinated by the turmoil of the place and the intensity of the labour process they decided to start this series.

Arguably, this fabrication workshop could be considered a sweatshop for art production. But this is a highly specialised craft and the artisans use specific techniques of hammering and polishing that take years to learn. The likes of these techniques cannot be found in Europe and even in China it is a dwindling skill.

Therefore, workers have to be recruited from all over the country.

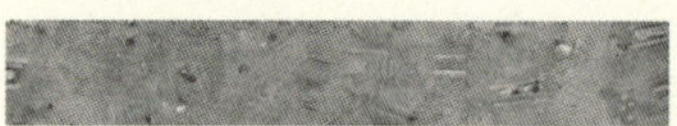

59 HUI'AN
Granite sculpture workshop in China
150 × 960 cm | 60" × 378"
35 × 225 cm | 14" × 89"

The city of Hui'an, in the province of Fujian in southeast China, has a long history of mining and sculpting granite. Katrin and Jens found themselves in a region that is dominated by stone-carving factories, where sculptures of various kinds are lined up along the streets. Artists from all over the world have their work manufactured here and shipped overseas to their final destinations in museums or galleries. The workshops manufacture anything from modern abstract sculptures to kitschy decorations. A layer of fine granite dust covers the streets and enters the houses. Stone carving is a very labour-intensive and even dangerous profession with the loud noises of hammering constantly in the background.

Although the Hui'an Chinese officially belong to the Han nationality, many aspects of their culture are unique among the people of China. In this picture, you can see some women wearing specific hats and scarves that are part of the traditional regional costume. These costumes have attracted the attention of both anthropologists and governmental censorship. The clothes give the wearer a regional identity, something that has largely been banned throughout the country. In the 20th century, most of the strenuous carving was done by female workers while the men were either fishing at sea or fighting in wars.

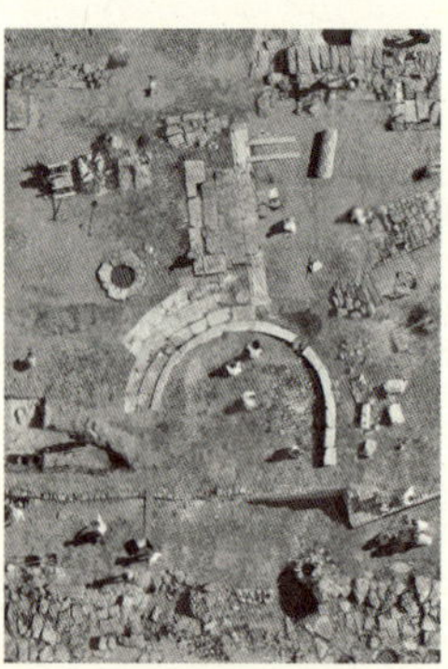

60 TROY
Archaeological excavation in Troy, Turkey
350 × 243 cm | 138" × 96"
173 × 120 cm | 68" × 47"

In Troy, the culture lies hidden in the earth, layered during centuries and re-cultivated through archaeological excavation. Troy is a mythical place, full of history and shrouded in mystery. The identity of Troy oscillates between epic tale and historical fact. Even today it is still unclear if the war and the famous ploy with the Trojan horse ever really happened. However, Homer's epic has become part of our cultural identity. The image shows only a small part of the huge and multiple-layered excavation site. It just looks like a large surface with stones where people are working and digging in the hot sun. Very much like the Trojan myth, it is unclear what kind of history has actually taken place in this dry and sandy landscape.

The culture is hidden in and under numerous layers of sand and stone and can only be revealed by excavation. Creating this picture was a personal trip for Katrin as her uncle, the highly respected archaeologist M. Osman Korfmann who passed away in 2005, dedicated his whole life to researching Troy.

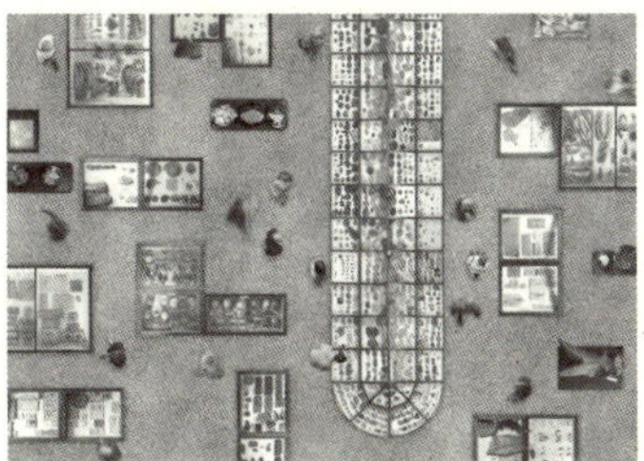

70   TEYLERS, HAARLEM
18th-century museum for the arts
and sciences in the Netherlands
300 × 430 cm | 118" × 170"
120 × 173 cm | 47" × 68"

Founded in 1784, the Teylers Museum is the first and oldest museum in the Netherlands. It is a museum for both art and science that displays artistic endeavours like paintings alongside scientific objects and paraphernalia. The long vitrine in the middle of the picture is unique and typical for the museum. The museum even has several fake artefacts on exhibit, a prank that malicious colleagues pulled on the collector and amateur-archaeologist Johann Beringer. As the picture is quite large you can see all the details of the fossils and skeletons. The vitrines, the objects, and the floor are all in black and white while the visitors are portrayed in colour. This is to emphasise the contrast between the history of the museum and the dynamics of the people present. This work is an interpretation of a classic display that shows the collecting and archiving of artefacts. It elucidates that art, or the perception of art, is not exclusively reserved for the process of conceiving or making but still happens in the 'afterlife' of objects.

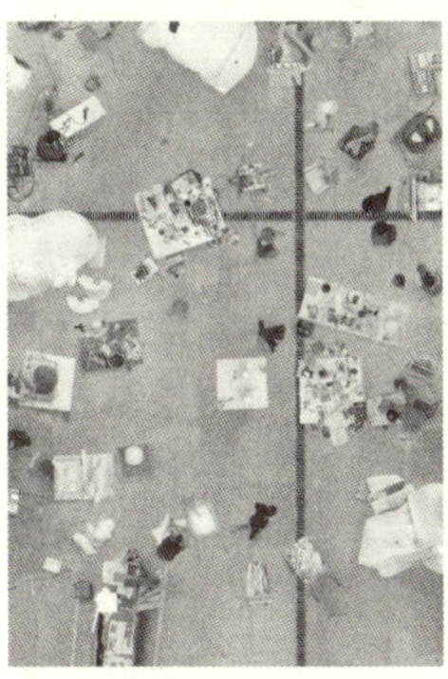

82   BILDHAUERWERKSTATT, BERLIN
Collaborative artists' studio space
in Germany
145 × 100 cm | 57" × 39 "

The Bildhauerwerkstatt in Berlin is a place where artists can rent a workshop and create with materials like metal, wood, stone, ceramics, plaster and plastic. It is situated in a hidden romantic industrial monument next to a little river in the neighbourhood of Wedding. The surface of the Werkstatt is 3600m2 in total with ceilings as high as 12 meters. Because the space is supported by the city, rent is affordable. There are not

many open studios like this in Berlin and Bildhauerwerkstatt is very popular and busy. The well-equipped workshops with their cooperative ambiance draw professional artists and amateurs alike and are purely designed to support the process of making. There is no room for presentations or exhibitions.

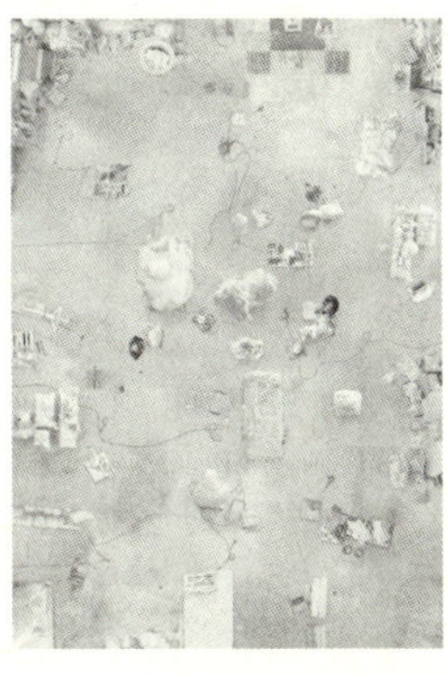

93   MARBLE, CARRARA
Marble production company in Italy
216 × 150 cm | 85" × 59"
173 × 120 cm | 68" × 47"

Carrara, in the northwest of Tuscany, Italy, is a city that is famous for its marble production. Since Roman times, Carrara has been the heart of the world's marble production, making the quarries one of the oldest industrial areas still in use. Even the one where Michelangelo chose the marble for his famous Pièta is still in use. The mountains in Carrera host about 600 marble quarries. In addition there are multiple marble museums and marble workspaces. This picture shows small traces of the region's grand history. In the far-left corner, the feet of a David replica are visible. One of the workers wears a hat folded from a newspaper, a typical costume feature worn by craftsmen from Carrara. Everything in the workspace is covered in fine white marble dust, merging the image into a monochrome tableau.

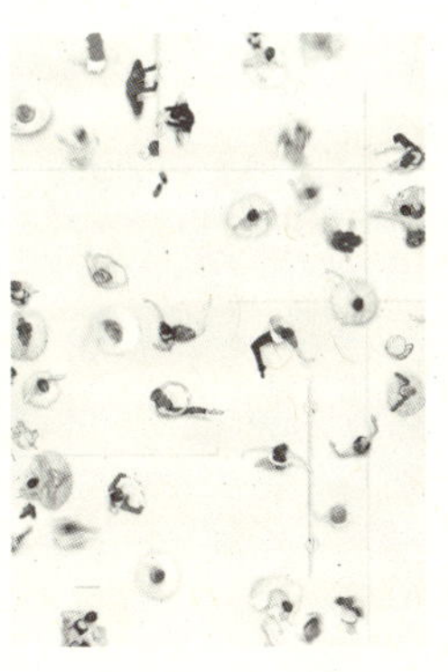

94   BALLET REHEARSAL, AMSTERDAM
Rehearsal of the Dutch National Ballet,
the Netherlands
145 × 100 cm | 57" × 39"

In Amsterdam, a rehearsal for the ballet piece Sleeping Beauty by the Dutch National Ballet is in full swing: from the stretching on the ground, to the exercises at the barre and finally the elegant poses and pirouettes of the corps and solo dancers. A ballet shoe is being laced, jackets and long trousers are being taken off and costumes are zipped up. There is a certain crescendo within the process of shedding layers of clothes as

part of the dynamics and rhythm of the rehearsal. In the picture, you can feel the movement of the dancers, but it is not yet fully coordinated. The lines and dots on the floor are codes that tell the dancers how and where to move. Some props that are used in the show, like flowers, are also part of the rehearsal scene. The practice and repetition of the dance until perfection are part of a production process. Despite the cleanliness and the assumed fragility, it is the hard physical labour that makes this workplace so fascinating.

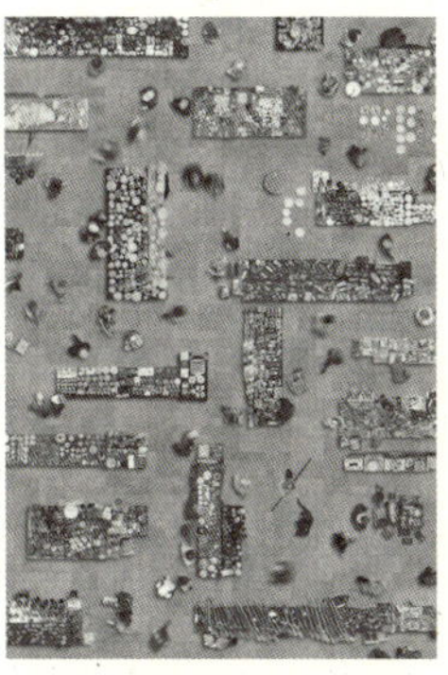

105   VERZAMELAARSJAARBEURS
Collectors Fair in Utrecht, the Netherlands
173 × 120 cm | 68" × 47"

Twice a year, people present and sell their collections of beloved objects here. The merchandise ranges from displayed ceramic and glass collections to more kitschy items like dozens of cuddly toys carefully arranged on a table, as if they were exhibits in a museum.

Back Stages eventually refers to the border of art, kitsch and design, and these themes are stressed in the image of the Verzamelaars-Jaarbeurs.

The objects we call kitsch may well be art in other countries. You can actually find many fascinating and valuable items at the fair. But its true worth is in the wonderful variety of the kinds of objects people cherish and find interesting enough to collect, show and share with others.

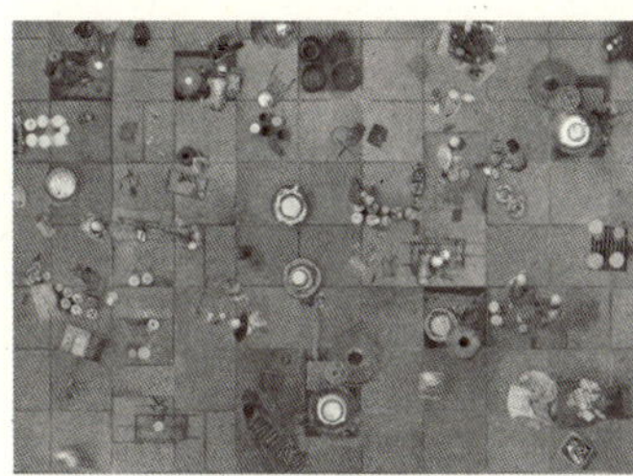

106   NIJHOF BEELDENSTORM, BRABANT
Bronze art foundry in the Netherlands
120 × 173 cm | 47" × 68"

This picture is a combination of two bronze art foundries in the Netherlands: De Smelterij in Veen and Beeldenstorm in Eindhoven. The latter is an open workspace where artists can work with different materials and techniques supported by a team of dedicated specialists. The former is a traditional family business, run by Hans and Marion Nijhof, that offers the full service of bronze casting; from mould making to patinated finishes. Katrin and Jens decided to merge images of the two companies into one picture to create a fragmented space that makes the process of bronze and aluminium casting appealing.

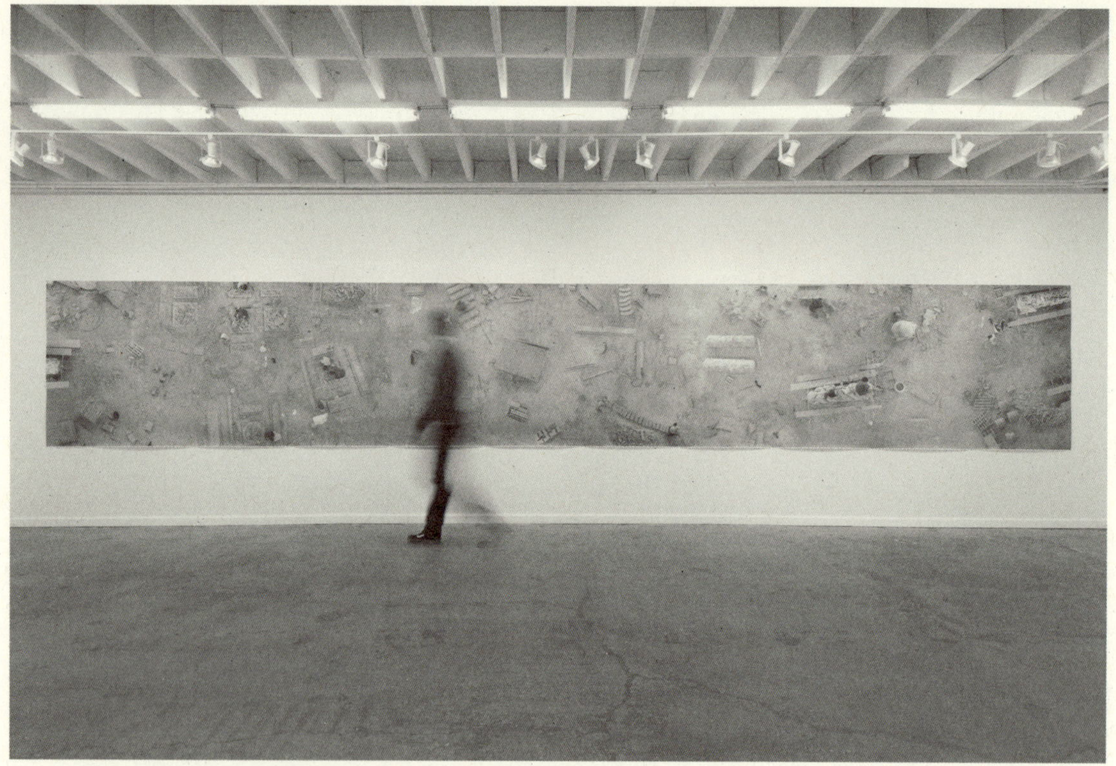

Kopeikin Gallery, Los Angeles

Big Art, Amsterdam

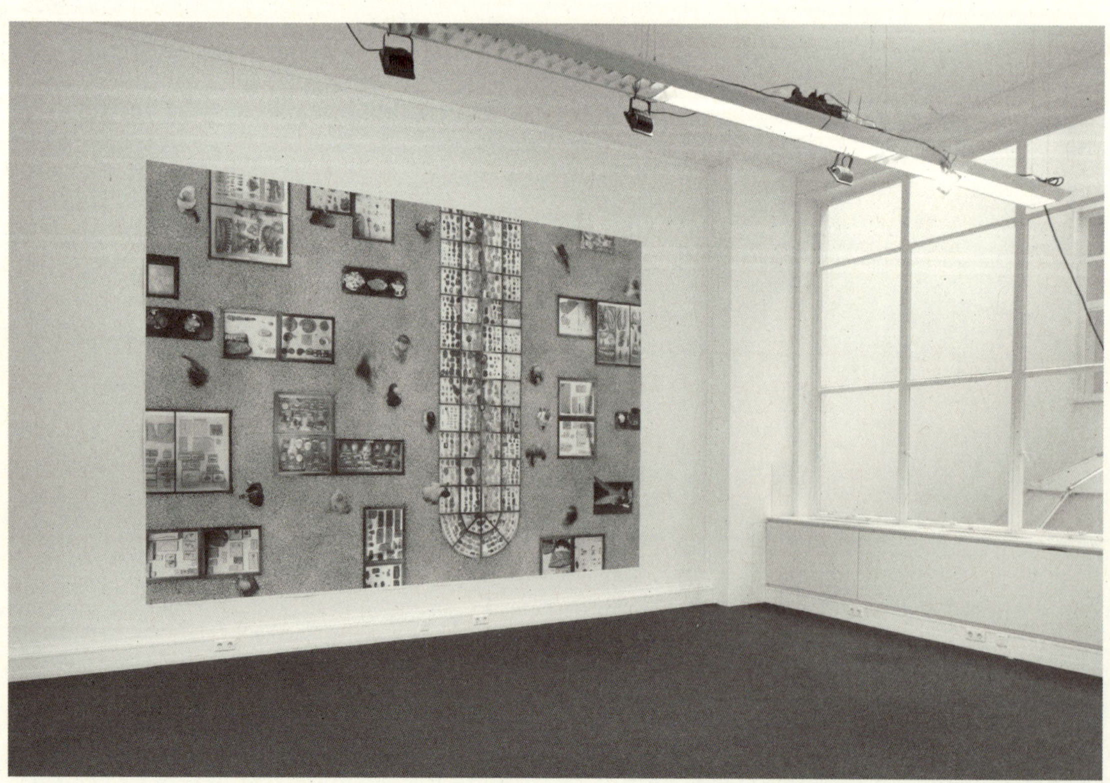

          INSTALLATION VIEW

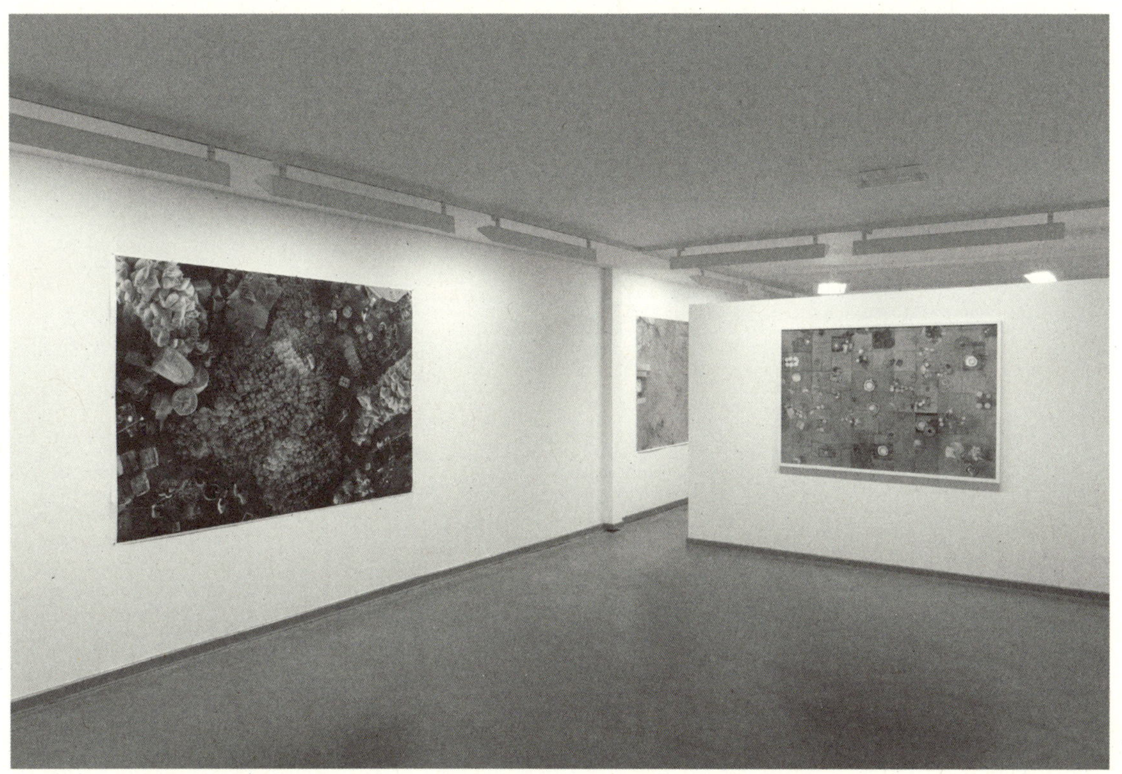

Onomatopee, Eindhoven

Onomatopee, Eindhoven

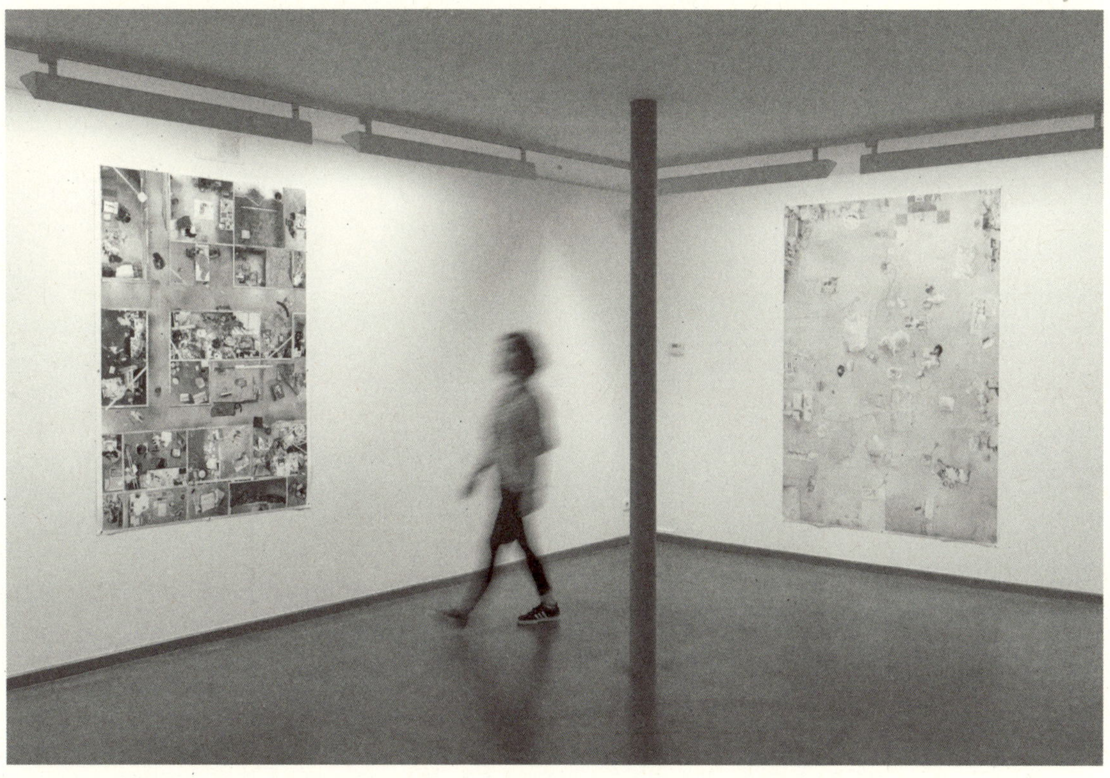

BIOGRAPHIES

KATRIN KORFMANN grew up in Berlin and has been living and working in Amsterdam since 1995. Her work includes photography and installations in public space that reveal a new perspective on social dynamics. Strongly aesthetic, her photographic images present an abstract of human interaction bound by the grid of everyday life. Time is an important determinant in her work, made visible through the presentation of different sequential incidents that have been registered within a given period and location, in one single spatial arrangement. The issue of responsibility for the existence of an image, the choice of the right moment and the framing that determines an image, also play an important role. Often using a vertical perspective, she is simultaneously zooming in and zooming out, creating a suggestion of distance and proximity at the same time. The artist carefully stages her images and depicts mysterious realities, which neither the eye, nor the artist's camera could have captured.

Katrin studied Photography at the Gerrit Rietveld Academie and continued her research during residencies at the Rijksakademie Amsterdam, Cittadellarte, Italy and the Chinese European Art Centre in Xiamen. Since the late 1990s, her work has been exhibited internationally in galleries, museums, public and alternative art spaces such as Kopeikin Gallery, Los Angeles, Kemper Museum of Contemporary Art, Kansas, and Aperture Foundation, New York, in the US; Frankfurter Kunstverein, Haus der Fotografie, Burghausen, and Akademie der Künste, Berlin, in Germany; International Canakkale Biennial, Turkey; Three Shadows Art Centre, Xiamen, China; Photography Museum Rotterdam, GEM Museum voor actuele Kunst, The Hague, and Teylers Museum, Haarlem, in the Netherlands. She won several awards for her work, including Radostar Prize by Biel/Bienne Festival of Photography, Switzerland; Prix de Rome (2nd prize) and the Esther Kroon Award in the Netherlands, and she received grants from international institutions like Mondriaan Fund; Robert Bosch and Würth Foundation; and Akademie der Künste Berlin. In addition to her practice as a visual artist, she is a tutor at the Royal Academy of Art in The Hague. Her work is represented in various private and corporate collections, for instance Bill and Christy Gautreaux, Twitter, Fidelity Investments Corporate Art Collection in the US; Würth Foundation and the Alison & Peter W. Klein Collection in Germany; and Drake Collection, AMC Art Collection, Bouwfonds Art Collection of Rabo Real Estate Group, ING Art Collection and European Patent Office in the Netherlands. She realized several commissions, for example for the Ministry of Finance, Rijksgebouwendienst, Schiphol Airport, University VUmc and Ronald McDonald Centre in the Netherlands; Ford in the US; and Stockholm County Council in Sweden.

JENS PFEIFER was born in Spain. He grew up in Germany and has been based in Amsterdam since 1988. His oeuvre comprises mainly sculptures and drawings that depict the paradoxical and distant relationships we have with our environment and fellow creatures, and highlight multiple means of expressing our cultural identity. The work has long been nourished from his personal narrative but increasingly contemplates other cultures and immanent socio-cultural correlations. Maintaining a consistent curiosity for the materiality of things, Jens is using glass, steel, plastics, ink and paper, or a camera to express his artistic narrative. Jens studied at the Royal College of Art in London and at the Gerrit Rietveld Academie in Amsterdam, where he currently holds the position of director of the Large Glass Department. Other teaching experiences cover academies and workshops worldwide, including Germany, Czech Republic, Denmark, Great Brittan, Lithuania, China, Israel and Turkey. In 2014 he co-initiated the temporary material - master programme for the Sandberg Institute in Amsterdam. Meanwhile he is strongly engaged in the organisation of a European platform for art education as founder and coordinator of The Glass Virus, Think Tank for educational strategies and perspectives. His work is exhibited internationally and is represented in a number of private and public collections, such as Museum Boijmans van Beuningen, Frans Hals Museum, De Nederlandsche Bank, Glas Museum Leerdam, AMC Collection, VSB Bank, Akzo Nobel Art Foundation and ABN/Amro Collection in the Netherlands; Museum Ebeltoft in Denmark; and Corning Museum, USA.

For the series **BACK STAGES**, Korfmann and Pfeifer collaborated for the first time since they became partners, nearly 20 years ago. Drawn from different angles of observation, both artists share a fascination for the manufacturing systems of art and culture and the valuation of work in the multifaceted process of making.

PAUL DE BRUYNE is a Belgian theatre maker, teacher and art critic. He has written numerous articles and books on the relationship of artistic craftmanship and societal developments. His theatrework has been produced in many countries all over the world.

COLOPHON / IMPRINT

Onomatopee 158

Back Stages
ISBN: 978-94-93148-06-2

Text contribution: Paul De Bruyne

Graphic design: Céline Hurka

Image editing: Katrin Korfmann and Jens Pfeifer

Translation text: Nanne op 't Ende,
other text by Josh Plough, Pernilla Ellens

Edition: 700

Typeface: Junior by Selina Bernet

Photography:
p. 120 by Katrin Korfmann and Jeff McLane
p. 121 by Blickfanger

Printing: Unicum / Gianotten, Tilburg

Made possible thanks to the generous financial
support of Mondriaan Fund and Jaap Harten Fonds.

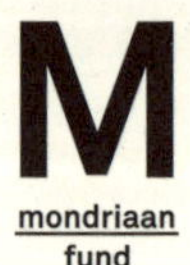 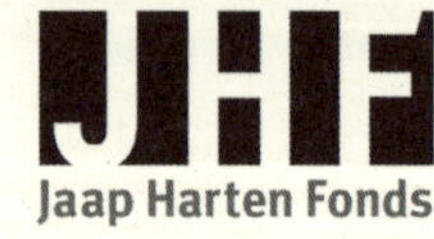

www.katrinkorfmann.com
www.jenspfeifer.org
www.celinehurka.com
www.onomatopee.net

We would like to express our appreciation for the help
and assistance in one or more productions to:

Céline Hurka, Jasmin Peco

Antoinette de Stigter — Art Affairs Amsterdam;
Paul Kopeikin — Kopeikin Gallery, Los Angeles;
Marianne van Tilborg — Galerie Lumen Travo, Amsterdam;
Galeri Andersson / Sandström, Stockholm;
Bau-Xi Photo, Toronto;
Nicole Löser — Whiteconcepts Berlin;
Christine van den Bergh — Bradwolff Projects

May Lee, Ineke Gudmundsson, Sigurdur Gudmundsson,
Zhiqiu Huang, Ye Qianfu, Kang You Teng, Jan Maruhn,
Steffen Hoppe, Ted Brandson, Richard Heideman, the
dancers from the National Ballet, Marion & Hans Nijhof,
Lex van Lith, Adam Etmanski, Willem Rieder, Yvonne
Dröge Wendel, Jurgen Bey, Teylers Museum, Cervietti
Franco, Nicola Stagetti, Andrei Carlo, Brunella Vatteroni,
Karim Zaidan, Rüstem Aslan, Wendy Rigter, Ruijgrok
Piëzografie, Zuzanna Zgierska, Susana Carvalho — Atelier
Carvalho Bernau, Selina Bernet, Margrit Korfmann-André

Onomatopee, Freek Lomme, Paul De Bruyne, Nanne
op t' Ende, Josh Plough, Pernilla Ellens

Our special thanks go to our beloved daughters Josefien
and Käthe for their patience and critical support.